STEAMY KITCHEN'S
healthy asian favorites :

STEAMY KITCHEN'S
healthy asian favorites

100 recipes that are fast, fresh, and simple enough for tonight's supper

JADEN HAIR

FOREWORD BY REE DRUMMOND

TEN SPEED PRESS
Berkeley

contents

foreword

I met Jaden Hair on the internet.

I just love saying that. And it's true. My first introduction to Jaden was stumbling onto her website, which—all the way back in the dark ages of 2007—was just as stunning as she was. I knew Jaden had been on television, and as a fledgling food blogger I was intimidated (and a bit awed) by her crisp, vivid photography and her undeniable gorgeousness. So I put her into the category of People I'll Admire From Afar, Thank You Very Much, never really imagining that we'd ever cross paths in real life.

By 2008, Jaden and I had struck up a friendship via email. Food blogging was a smaller community back then and we wound up consulting with each other about this and that. A year or so later, we wound up together at a food conference. Elise Bauer (of simplyrecipes.com), Jaden, and I had crammed ourselves into the back of a small taxi in San Francisco, and somewhere along the way our driver ran a red light and we were almost completely sideswiped by another car. We always (somewhat nervously!) joke about that harrowing experience being the first time we met. But in fact, that night was the beginning of a forever friendship.

That's *how* I know Jaden. Now let me tell you what I *know* about Jaden. She's ridiculously full of life, with a laugh that can be heard four states away. She's up for anything—I've never proposed a plan or a get-together that Jaden wasn't excited about. She's unfathomably creative. And she's an accomplished businesswoman, with ideas and ambition that would wear me out within a week. But most of all, she loves her husband Scott and their two boys, Andrew and Nathan, more than life itself.

And then there's Jaden's food, which is not only magazine-worthy and photogenic, but also tremendously delicious. Her attention to detail—not just in how the food looks, but how it tastes—means every bite you put in your mouth will be a transcendent experience. I remember whipping up Jaden's Beef with Broccoli for the first time and being astounded at not only how simple it was to prepare and how yummy it was, but how perfectly thought-out all the quantities of ingredients were. Where I would have sloshed in soy sauce and thrown in other ingredients willy-nilly, Jaden allowed for a precise amount of soy sauce, cornstarch, and other ingredients so that not a single drop went to waste or was unused. This is a bonus of Jaden's recipes: You know you'll only use what you need.

In *Steamy Kitchen's Healthy Asian Favorites*, Jaden brings down to earth all the irresistible Asian recipes that many of us love ordering in restaurants but could never imagine making at home. Everything from a simple Egg Drop and Tomato Soup all the way up to a Salmon Honey Teriyaki and even an impressive Chinese Hot Pot Party is presented in a straightforward way, using ingredients that most anyone can get at a supermarket. Simple instructions for making luscious stocks, perfect steamed rice, and yummy dumplings ensure that the basics are covered.

As Jaden's friend, I loved her first cookbook, which was released a few years ago. But as a home cook and lover of simple Asian recipes, I am absolutely devouring this one. It makes Asian cooking possible for real home cooks like me, and it challenges me to tackle new frontiers in my kitchen.

But most of all, it inspires me.

And knowing Jaden like I do, I'm pretty sure that will make her day.

Ree Drummond
The Pioneer Woman

introduction

healthy asian favorites outside the take-out box

Did you know that we humans have about 10,000 taste buds? No wonder we enjoy eating so much! As a recipe developer and lover of food, I feel like it's my job to design dishes that take full advantage of every bite, pinging as many of those 10,000 taste buds as possible.

So push aside the old standby take-out classics, like greasy kung pao and starchy egg rolls. There's so much more to Asian cuisine than the pedestrian chicken teriyaki. And General Tso's got nothin' new up his sleeve, either. I say it's time for a little innovation—to be creative, and combine Asian spices with American and other ethnic favorites.

Instead of just Korean beef bulgogi grilled and served over rice, I'll show you Korean Beef Bites (page 64) on a crunchy, airy rice cracker topped with fiery kimchi as a fifteen-minute appetizer. Instead of the traditional Chinese steamed whole fish, I'll combine fish fillets baked in parchment with the same authentic Chinese herbs and seasonings. Latin gazpacho gets a jolt from Thai chilies, a healthy squeeze of lime, and splash of fish sauce. Traditional oil-heavy and meat-rich Sichuanese Dan Dan Mien (page 177) gets considerably lighter with lots of napa cabbage and just enough ground chicken.

This book is all about learning to cook healthy foods in a modern Asian style. I'll show you how to make recipes that you and your family will look forward to eating, are easy on the pocketbook, and light on the waistline.

COOKING HEALTHY MEANS FOUR THINGS IN THE STEAMY KITCHEN:

1. Holding back on the dense, high-calorie sauces and instead focusing on fresh herbs and fragrant spices, and using a combination of what I call the "Five S's" (salty, sweet, sour, savory, and spicy) that are used in authentic Asian cooking.

2. Learning cooking techniques that cut down on the use of a lot of fats, oils, and sugars. Correct stir-frying techniques only use a couple teaspoons of cooking oil per dish.

3. Using meats more sparingly, following how Asians normally use meats as more of a condiment than the star attraction of the meal.

4. Focusing on recipes that are naturally gluten-light or entirely gluten-free. Simple substitutions are always provided, like substituting rice noodles for wheat noodles.

my story

Since the day I was born, food and family have been my everything. In fact, I even think that food and family are one and the same. I remember, in detail, our daily family dinners in Hong Kong at a big round glass table covered with a thin, disposable white plastic tablecloth (we must have been really messy eaters?), with no less than five different dishes that we shared family style.

Spending my early years in Hong Kong is one of the greatest influences on my palate and cooking style. The island is surrounded by some of the best seafood in the world and locals celebrate food that is same-day fresh.

I loved shopping in the afternoon with my Gong Gong (maternal grandpa) or Kau-Fu (uncle) Patrick at the wet markets, picking out live seafood, fresh produce, and maybe a bit of meat to cook that night. Lunch was something simple—usually we ordered from a nearby restaurant within walking distance. My family's shops were surrounded by dozens of lunch choices within a two-block radius. Fast food wasn't about hamburgers, but rather steaming-hot vegetables with soy sauce rice or maybe a noodle soup with roast duck. Fast food wasn't about how cheap or how fast you could go through a drive-through lane, but rather how fast the delivery boy could walk-run your order without spilling the basket's contents.

When my family moved to North Platte, Nebraska, food took on the role of ambassador. Many of my Dad's co-workers' wives became good friends with Mom, teaching her homemade pie crusts, the art of the American casserole and what to do with the plentiful zucchini and corn from the garden. My love of sharing recipes came from watching my Mom learn how to cook American dishes from our neighbors.

I remember good friends Alice and Walt Guenthner's backyard full of cherry and apple trees. During harvest, the adults would climb up the ladders to pick and we children would scour the grass looking for fallen fruit.

After cooking lessons, Dad would read the recipe from the cookbook, translating it into Cantonese for Mom who would then handwrite the recipe in Chinese characters. Mom still has an old wooden box with index cards packed with recipes from those days.

When I first started SteamyKitchen.com several years ago, my parents came to visit and brought a stack of recipe cards. Mom and I spent a couple afternoons sitting on the couch—she would translate her Chinese recipes into English (errr . . . . Chinglish) for me to type on my laptop.

Now, I'm sharing some of those recipes with you.

My love of Asian food and flavors is the basis of everything I create in the kitchen. Even when I'm cooking non-Asian food, I'm thinking of the balance of salty, sweet, savory, sour, and spicy in every bite. Can you imagine all those notes singing on your tongue? Your taste buds are so happy that it eliminates the need for oily, fatty, and heavy textures.

In this book, I celebrate healthful Asian eating with recipes that have nothing to do with counting calories. The natural and authentic recipes from across Asia are all about showcasing the best of fresh vegetables, the lively array of spices and condiments, and what I call the five S's: salty, sweet, savory, sour, and spicy.

With these recipes, you'll be able to feed your family and friends healthful, light meals with vibrant natural flavors!

about our homestead

The idea of living on a five-acre homestead is pretty ambitious, especially for a city girl like me, who spent most of her years in the hustle and bustle of Los Angeles and San Francisco.

When we first moved to Florida, we lived near a major transportation artery where semi-trucks would rumble back and forth between the inland orange orchard and the freeway. The trucks pulled open trailers filled to the top with oranges picked hours earlier. Once in a while, if the truck turned too quickly or if the wind was especially harsh, an orange or two would fall out of the truck onto the road.

When Andrew was three years old, I asked him, "Where do oranges come from?" His reply was kinda cute at first, "A truck!"

MY FIRST FOOD MEMORY

Food lovers always seem to get asked these two questions: What's your first food memory? What's your ideal last meal?

Is the meaning of life bookended by our first and last meals?

I say not!

I was a late teether and I'm pretty sure I'll go out with no teeth, too. Gumming food isn't my finest food moment, right?

But I know you're curious, so I'll answer. My last meal (with teeth!) would be street food in Hong Kong. Grilled skewers of squid with tentacles curled up, thin slices of charred cha-sui (roast pork), deep-fried, crackly-skin tofu slathered in hot chile sauce, and freshly made wontons that float like clouds in soup. Can you tell I love savory foods?

My first meal memory is nothing to brag about. Mushed something or other. But my first *favorite* food memory is with my Gong Gong (maternal grandpa). He used to own a couple of women's clothing shops in Hong Kong, and some mornings I'd go to work with him at the shop. My days were a little princess's

dream—trying on pretty jewelry, hats, lacey shawls, and tiptoeing in fancy high heels. Upstairs in the attic of the shop was my hiding place. Hiding amongst the industrial sewing machines for alterations and the maze of clothing racks of apparel was magic.

The seamstress kept me company and gave me scraps of shimmery fabrics to play with. I dressed my dolls with these scraps, pretending they were fancy evening gowns.

During lunchtime, Gong Gong would take my hand and we'd walk to eat lunch. There were so many choices! The shop was in the middle of a popular retail and open-market location at the Prince Edward subway stop. We'd pass by the roasted chestnut vendors during the winter (page 83), the newspaper stand that sold candies and young coconut water, and several fresh fruit carts before reaching the heart of the restaurant row. Roast pork over rice was my favorite. Gong Gong always made sure to tell them to put extra yummy sweet sauce on my rice.

Gong Gong and I also loved to eat dim sum, and sometimes we'd meet with my Uncle Patrick for lunch. People eat fast in Hong Kong. Dim sum places are very efficient in seating, taking your order, cooking, serving, and, of course, calculating your check. There's simply too many people to serve! Either you're waiting for a table or quickly darting your chopsticks from plate to mouth while an impatient customer is standing behind your chair, tapping their foot signaling for you to hurry up and finish.

Within 30 seconds of sitting down, the waiter would already have a pot of hot tea at our table and dim sum cart pushers would be hawking the goodies in their cart, "Cha sui bao! Cha sui bao!" *Steamed bbq pork buns!*, "Har Gow! Sui Mai!" *Steamed shrimp dumplings! Pork dumplings!*

We'd eat until we were stuffed. Then the servers would usher us out so that they could seat the next customers.

So my lifelong food adventures begin and end in Hong Kong.

Uh . . . wait. There was something seriously wrong with my kid thinking oranges grow on trucks! I'm a food professional! I'm a cookbook author! How embarrassing! I needed to do something about this situation.

I began taking my kids to farmer's markets, and we started growing a few of our own vegetables in our little patch of a backyard. But I wanted to do more. What if we moved out to more land and started our own little homestead? Andrew and Nathan loved the idea.

The boys and I had big plans. The property we bought was five acres, enough space to run naked through the yard and nobody would notice. We wanted chickens, pigs, goats, fruit tree orchard, a hydroponic garden and all the fun urban farmer toys.

Scott reluctantly went along with the plan. He's certainly more of a city boy than a country boy, having grown up in Buffalo, New York. Animal husbandry just didn't fit in his vocabulary of fun, but slowly, the boys and I eased him into the idea of keeping chickens.

It took a couple of months for Scott to warm up to Oreo, Fire Flapper, Frenzy, Shelby and Olivia Superstar (the kids had fun naming the chickens), and the idea of designing and building a "palatial" chicken coop was all Scott's idea.

We now have ten hens, producing anywhere between six and nine eggs a day, most of which we give away to friends. Our pond in the back is fully stocked with tilapia and blue gill, and our boys will go fishing for that night's dinner.

The garden has evolved slowly, each year it get a little bigger and we add on more raised beds. We grow all varieties of herbs, more tomatoes than we know what to do with, zucchini, eggplant, okra, bok choy, Chinese broccoli, peas, beans, Japanese cucumbers, and much more. Our next experiment is installing an aquaponic system!

As for the fruits, we haven't planted our little orchard of oranges and tropical fruits yet. But you can be sure that Andrew now knows where oranges come from!

about blogging

In December 2005, Nathan had just turned one and Andrew was two and a half years old. Scott was running our small computer repair business by day and then after dinner, he was a professional online poker player by night. Me? I was going absolutely crazy.

At this point in the story, I know you're saying, "Back up, girl. Did you say professional poker player?!" And you're probably imagining a typical poker pro, with the hat, dark sunglasses, hoodie, and stacks of multicolored chips on a felt green table.

Exactly that. Except without the hat, glasses, hoodie, and chips.

Insert into your imagination a massive desk, three computers (one is a backup computer in case the main one crashes), a $1,000 leather computer chair with built-in massager, three twenty-one-inch flat screen monitors, and an extra air conditioning unit to keep the room cool (all those electronics produce a lot of heat).

One monitor is divided into four separate sections—each section featuring a different poker game. Scott plays four games at the same time. The second screen is a custom poker stats computer program that he designed himself. At any given point in time, he knows what percentage of hands he's won with pocket 10's and knows how many times the player on the right has gone all-in pre-flop. The third screen is to chat with me.

As you know, running a small business is no easy thing, especially one with lots of overhead like our computer repair business. Poker was our paycheck for nearly four years. Those were wild times.

Okay, now that I've satisfied your curiosity, back to me and how I started blogging.

Those evenings, when Scott would be playing poker, I'd find company in reading food blogs like David Lebovitz in Paris (www.davidlebovitz.com). They were my companions until 4am, if it was a good night for Scott. Poker wives understand this. The later a husband comes to bed, the better—it means he's deep in the money in a tournament!

It wasn't until February 2007 that I actually decided to start my own food blog, instead of just being a voyeur of others, and SteamyKitchen.com was born. The site documented recipes that my mom would dictate to me over the phone.

In the early days, readers of the blog were just family members and a handful of friends. Within a couple of months, I had grown a steady base of readers seeking authentic Asian recipes. By month six, the site had been mentioned in the press and featured on popular food sites, I was cooking on television regularly, and a book deal was in negotiations. My first book, *The Steamy Kitchen Cookbook*, hit the shelves two years later.

Operating a popular food blog requires commitment, time, and energy. The blossoming business grew and grew and grew like Jack's beanstalk! It became much more than just sharing recipes on a web page. It became a full-time business. Scott sold the computer business and started helping run the web site. If I am "Steamy Kitchen" then he's the "dot com" of the business.

about the photography

With the exception of the fortune cookies (on page 201), every single recipe in this book was photographed by yours truly. Part of my process of creating recipes is the visual element—the food that I make has to look amazing as well as taste delicious!

When I first started the blog, my photo studio was a brilliantly simple three-dollar foam board from the office supply store, a TV tray, and an entry-level dSLR camera. Food photography isn't difficult, especially if you have a good eye for styling a plate of food and abundant natural light.

In my home now, we've built a photo studio that I use to store the hundreds of plates, bowls, chopsticks, platters, cups, glasses, and linens that I've collected. I have a lot of fun picking up one or two pieces of dishware every time I travel. The photos in this book were shot with a Canon 5D Mark II, a 100mm macro lens, and a sturdy tripod. The camera is tethered to my iMac, so that I can immediately see the photo seconds after I click.

For the book, I enlisted the help of crazy-talented Todd and Diane of White on Rice Couple (www.whiteonricecouple.com) and Jenna of Eat Live Run (www .eatliverun.com). We shot the majority of the photos in a span of four days. Jenna was the queen of chop-chop-chopping all the vegetables and herbs; Todd was the master cook, following my recipes; Diane helped me choose linens and dishware for styling; and I styled and photographed the food. Scott was our technical support to make sure the connection, computer and printer were operating smoothly and the boys were our taste testers. Coco, our dog, stood guard.

soups

ASIAN MOMS EXPRESS THEIR LOVE through homemade soup—my mom did and still does. When we were growing up, at least three times a week, Mom would simmer soup from scratch, whether it was from pork, chicken, or vegetables.

I try to do the same for my family, but a thrice weekly pot of soup from scratch is quite ambitious (trust me, I know). I've tested every single type of contraption and gadget created for making home-made soups easier—pressure cookers, slow cookers, thermos pots, rice cookers, and electric kettles. Half of those gadgets are stashed somewhere in the garage, and I always come back to the basic pot on the stove. Some of my soups are made from scratch, but most of my soup is "cheater soup." It took me nine years of therapy to accept this, so let me save you the time, trouble, and expense and tell you: it's okay. I give you permission to use store-bought broth.

Just make sure you look for organic, low-sodium brands. And then load up your soup with tons of fresh goodies like spinach, mush-rooms, seafood, and whatever else makes you happy.

Soup makes people happy.
Eat more soup for world peace!

mom's chicken stock

One of the very first things I learned from Mom was how to make her clean, clear, and rich chicken stock. Her secret is to boil the chicken bones hard for 3 minutes to dislodge any scuz, scum, blood, and yuck that's hiding in the bones, meat, or skin. The boiling action scrubs the bones. You'll discard all of that scuzzy water, rinse the bones, and fill the pot again with clean, cool water. Don't worry, all the flavor is still in the bones and meat! Try this method and you'll be rewarded with the best, cleanest-tasting chicken stock. MAKES 4 QUARTS

4 pounds chicken bones, hacked into 2- to 3-inch sections, exposing the insides of the bones as much as possible
1 (4-inch) piece of fresh ginger, cut into coins
8 cloves garlic, smashed
8 green onions, green parts only, cut into thirds
1 small handful fresh cilantro (coriander) stems

Bring a large stockpot filled with water to a boil. When it reaches a boil, add the chicken bones. Keep the heat on high and boil the bones for 3 minutes. Pour out the water and rinse the bones. Add the rest of the ingredients as well as enough water to cover the bones by 2 inches. If you are using a whole chicken (not just bones), then fill with enough water to cover by 4 inches. Bring to a boil and immediately turn the heat to low and simmer for 1½ to 3 hours, skimming the surface periodically. The surface of the stock should be barely bubbling. Alternatively, you can put all the ingredients into a slow cooker or pressure cooker. (Follow the manufacturer's instructions for making stock.)

Strain the stock and discard the solids. After the soup cools, store in the refrigerator for up to 5 days or pour into a sealable freezer bag and lay flat in the freezer.

Best chicken soup ever!

vegetable stock

The secret to rich vegetable stock is to chop and sauté the vegetables in a little bit of oil before adding the water. This extra 3 minute step makes a world of difference. I also like to add dried Chinese black mushrooms to the stock for a bit more body and hearty flavor. MAKES 4 QUARTS

1 tablespoon canola oil
3 carrots, peeled and sliced on the diagonal
3 celery stalks, sliced on the diagonal
1/2 onion, cut into large chunks
3 dried Chinese black mushrooms, washed well, or substitute with 1/4 cup sliced fresh shiitake mushrooms
1 (4-inch) piece of fresh ginger, cut into 1/8-inch-thick coins
8 cloves garlic, peeled and smashed
8 green onions, cut into thirds
1 small handful (about 1/2 ounce) fresh cilantro stems and/or leaves
4 quarts water

Add the oil to a large stockpot set over medium-high heat. When the oil is hot, add all the ingredients except the water and saute for 3 minutes. Add the water. Bring to a boil and immediately turn the heat to low. Simmer for 30 minutes to 1 hour, skimming the surface periodically. Strain and discard solids.

seafood stock

The tricky part of making seafood stock is to make sure that it doesn't taste too fishy. You can use fish bones, fish meat, shrimp shells, crab shells, and even lob- ster shells for the stock. Fry the bones and shells in a bit of cooking oil first to mel- low out the strong fishy taste and to give the stock a deeper, rounder flavor.

MAKES 4 QUARTS

1 tablespoon canola oil
Seafood bones and shells to fill a 4-quart freezer bag
1 (4-inch) piece of fresh ginger, cut into 1/8-inch- thick coins
8 cloves garlic, peeled and smashed
8 green onions, cut into thirds
1 small handful (about 1/2 ounce) fresh cilantro stems and/or leaves
4 quarts water

In a large stockpot over medium heat, add the oil. When the oil is hot, add the bones and shells and saute for 2 to 3 minutes, until the shells turn pink and the bones are white. Add the remaining ingredients. Bring to a boil and immediately turn the heat to low. Simmer for 30 minutes to 1 hour, skimming the surface periodically. Strain and discard the solids.

meat stock

As with Mom's Chicken Stock (page 10), you'll want to do a hard boil of the bones first, discard the water and scum, rinse the bones, and then proceed to make the stock. I know it's an extra step, but you'll be rewarded with the richest-tasting and clearest stock ever. If you don't have bones, that's fine, just use pork meat, like Boston butt.

MAKES 4 QUARTS

4 pounds meat and bones, a combination of boneless pork meat, pork bones, or beef bones
1 (4-inch) piece of fresh ginger, thinly sliced
8 cloves garlic, peeled and smashed
8 green onions, cut into thirds
1 small handful (about 1/2 ounce) fresh cilantro stems and/or leaves

Bring a large stockpot filled with water to a boil. When it reaches a boil, add the meat and bones. Keep the heat on high and boil for 3 minutes. Pour out the water (you'll notice a lot of scum) and rinse the bones. Return the bones to the pot and add the rest of the ingredients as well as enough water to cover the meat and bones by 4 inches.

Bring to a boil and immediately turn the heat to low and simmer for 1½ to 2 hours, skimming the surface periodically. The surface of the stock should be barely bubbling. Alternatively, you can put all the ingredients into a slow cooker or pressure cooker. (Follow the instructions provided with your appliance for making stock.)

Strain the stock and discard the solids.

dashi

The basis of many Japanese dishes is the dashi, which is made from dried seaweed (kombu) and dried bonito fish flakes. Here, I've given you three ways to make dashi. MAKES 5 CUPS

5 cups water
6 (8-inch) piece of kombu
2 large handfuls dried bonito flakes (about 3 cups)

Gently wipe the kombu with a damp towel to clean (do not rinse). In a large stockpot, add the water and the kombu, bring to a boil. Turn the heat to low and stir in the bonito flakes. Let simmer for 5 minutes. Remove from heat and let sit for 10 minutes. Strain the stock. Discard the bonito but keep the kombu. (You can reuse several times.)

SHORTCUT DASHI WITH INSTANT DASHI: In a stockbot bring 5 cups water to a boil. Tun off heat and stir in 2 teaspoons instant dashi (Hondashi).

FOR THE SHORTCUT DASHI WITH SOUP BASE IN MESH BAGS, please follow package directions.

miso soup

Add your choice of ingredients, such as green onions, sliced mushrooms, seaweed, or whatever floats your tofu. SERVES 4

5 cups prepared dashi (page 14)
4 tablespoons miso paste

Bring dashi to a low simmer. Add ingredients of your choice and cook 1-2 minutes or until cooked through. Turn off heat and whisk in miso paste.

egg drop and tomato soup

Egg drop soup really should be renamed—have you ever tried dropping an egg in boiling soup? Plunk! Splat! Instead of just cracking an egg into the stock, the secret to silky strands of egg is to first beat the eggs in a small bowl. Then, gently and slowly, swirl in the egg in a very thin stream. Gently. It's a kind and happy soup. SERVES 4

1 quart vegetable stock (page 11) or organic low-sodium chicken stock, divided
2 eggs, lightly beaten
1 large tomato, cut into 8 wedges
1 green onion, minced
Salt and white pepper
1/4 teaspoon toasted sesame oil

Measure 2 tablespoons of the stock and whisk it with the beaten eggs. Set aside. Bring the remaining stock to a boil. Add the tomatoes and simmer for 2 minutes. In a very thin stream, drizzle in the egg in a large, circular motion. This creates the "egg drop." Simmer for 1 minute to let the egg cook and set. Do not stir the soup until the egg sets.

Add the green onion and season with salt and pepper. Stir in the sesame oil.

Wispy strands of egg . . .

thai tom yum soup

This recipe includes two versions of this classic Thai dish. The first one uses galangal, lemongrass, and kaffir lime leaves; great for those who live near an Asian market and can readily get those ingredients (you lucky ducks!). The second version is for those who don't and instead uses easy to find supermarket ingredients. SERVES 4

VERSION 1

2 quarts vegetable stock (page 11)
1 thumb-sized piece of galangal or ginger, thinly sliced on the diagonal
3 kaffir lime leaves, each leaf torn a couple of times
1 fresh Thai red chile, sliced in half lengthwise, seeds discarded
1 lemongrass stalk, bottom 4 inches only, sliced in half lengthwise
2 tablespoons fish sauce
1 teaspoon sugar
1 lime, halved
1 handful fresh mushrooms, sliced
1 large tomato, cut into 8 wedges
6 ounces firm tofu, cut into small cubes
1/2 carrot, shaved with vegetable peeler
Cilantro, for garnish

In a large saucepan or stockpot, add the stock, galangal, lime leaves, and chile. Smash the lemongrass stalk with the side of your knife to release its aroma and flavor. Add the lemongrass to the stock. Turn heat to low and simmer for 15 minutes.

Discard the solids, keeping the chile if you want a spicier soup. Whisk in the fish sauce and the sugar. Squeeze in the lime.

Add the mushrooms, tomato, carrot, and tofu to the stock and return to a simmer for 2 minutes. Remove from heat and top with fresh cilantro to serve.

....

1 lime
2 quarts vegetable stock (page 11)
1 thumb-sized piece of ginger, thinly sliced
1 fresh chile, sliced in half lengthwise, seeds discarded
2 tablespoons fish sauce
1 teaspoon sugar
1 handful fresh mushrooms, sliced
1 tomato, cut into wedges
1/2 carrot, shaved with a vegetable peeler
6 ounces firm tofu, cut into small cubes
Cilantro, for garnish

Using a vegetable peeler, peel three large sections of skin from the lime (avoiding the bitter white pith). Set aside the lime to use later. Use your fingers to twist the peel and release its fragrance and oils. Place the lime peels in a large pot along with the vegetable stock, ginger, and chile. Turn heat to low and bring to a simmer. Let simmer for 15 minutes. Discard the solids, keeping the chile if you want a spicier soup. Whisk in the fish sauce and the sugar. Cut the peeled lime in half and squeeze the juice into the stock.

Add the mushrooms, tomato, carrot, and tofu to the stock and return to a simmer for 2 minutes. Remove from the heat and top with fresh cilantro to serve.

Yum yum for Tom Yum!

healing chicken ginger soup

When I'm sick, this is the only soup I want: real chicken soup that soothes sore throats and nourishes the body. The key to clear soup is to boil the chicken hard for a few minutes to release all of the scum from the bones and skin. You'll be surprised at how much scum rises to the surface! Dump all of that water and refill the pot with fresh water along with the parboiled bones. I've left the amount of salt and pepper up to you—sometimes when you're sick, your taste buds change.

For even better flavor, instead of plain salt, I add a few splashes of fish sauce to give it a balanced, savory flavor. The fish sauce not only gives the soup a more Asian taste, but it also adds umami and depth of flavor that plain salt can't.

Mom always taught me to use cilantro stems when making soup, reserving the leaves for garnish or other stir-fry dishes, where pretty matters. The stems have just as much flavor! **MAKES 1 QUART**

2 pounds chicken wings, backs, bones, or meat

1 (4-inch) piece of fresh ginger

4 green onions, cut into 4-inch pieces

1 small bunch cilantro (you'll use all the stems and a few of the leaves for garnish)

Salt and freshly ground black pepper

Cut the ginger into thin slices, about
$1/8$ inch thick. Use the side of your chef's knife
to smash each slice to break its fibers and
release its flavors.

In a large pot, add the chicken wings and fill
with water to cover by 1 inch. Bring to a boil
over high heat. Boil hard for 5 minutes, until
you see quite a bit of scum on the surface of the
water.

Place a large colander in the sink. Carefully
bring the pot to the sink and drain into the colander, discarding the water. Rinse the chicken
wings with clean water and place back into the
pot, along with the ginger, green onion, and the
cilantro stems. Refill pot with clean water and
return to stove. Bring to a boil and turn heat to
a low simmer for 45 minutes.

Strain the soup and discard all the solids.
Season with salt and pepper; garnish with some
of the cilantro leaves to serve.

Like a warm hug.

hot and sour soup

This is the soup for you if you like it spicy! And if you have a cold, it will clear your sinuses right up. The secret ingredients are Chinese black vinegar and white pepper. Chinese black vinegar is aged vinegar that's tangy and slightly sweet—if you don't have it, substitute with non-aged balsamic vinegar. Just make sure that the balsamic isn't too sweet. You want the tang to shine!

Ground white pepper is used in lot of Chinese cooking, sometimes for aesthetic reasons—no black flecks in an otherwise light-colored dish—and sometimes for practical reasons—white pepper is powdered, which makes it easier to blend into a dish. SERVES 4 TO 6

1/3 pound ground chicken, turkey, or pork

1 teaspoon plus 1 to 2 tablespoons low-sodium
    soy sauce

1 teaspoon Chinese rice wine

1/2 teaspoon toasted sesame oil

Pinch of sugar

2 teaspoons cornstarch

4 cups fat-free vegetable (page 11) or chicken stock
    (page 10)

1/2 cup shiitake mushrooms, thinly sliced

1/2 cup canned or fresh bamboo shoots, julienned

10 ounces firm tofu, cut into 3/4-inch cubes

1 to 2 tablespoons Chinese black vinegar or non-aged
    balsamic vinegar

1 teaspoon freshly ground white pepper, plus more
    as needed

1 green onion, very thinly sliced on diagonal

Combine the meat, 1 teaspoon of the soy sauce, rice wine, sesame oil, sugar, and cornstarch in a large bowl. Mix well. Let marinate at room temperature for 10 minutes. Bring the stock to a boil in a large saucepan over high heat. Add the meat mixture and stir, breaking up with the back of a spoon. Let the liquid return to a boil, then reduce the heat to medium and add the mushrooms, bamboo shoots, and tofu. Cook for 3 to 5 minutes, or until the pork is cooked through and the mushrooms have softened.

Season the soup with the remaining 1 tablespoon soy sauce, black vinegar, and white pepper. Stir, taste, and add more soy, black vinegar, and/or white pepper as needed. Divide among individual bowls; garnish each portion with green onion.

tofu-mushroom miso soup

Want to know the secret to Asian eternal youth and longevity? Soup for breakfast! The Chinese enjoy hearty soups and porridges in the morning; and in Japan, a traditional breakfast includes miso soup. This is my power breakfast: quick miso soup with tofu, fresh vegetables, sliced mushrooms, and an egg stirred in. SERVES 4

4 cups dashi (page 14) or vegetable stock (page 11)
6 ounces firm tofu, cubed
4 ounces fresh mushrooms, sliced
1 handful leafy vegetables, like baby bok choy, napa cabbage, spinach, or kale, coarsely chopped
1 egg, whisked
2 tablespoons chopped green onion
4 tablespoons miso paste

In a saucepan, bring the dashi to a boil. Add the tofu, mushrooms, and vegetables. While stirring the dashi, slowly pour in the whisked egg. Cook for 2 minutes. Remove from the heat.

Ladle about ½ cup of the hot dashi into a bowl with the miso paste. Use a fork or whisk to blend the miso paste. Pour all of the miso into the pot and stir gently. Top with green onions and serve immediately.

Pssst . . . it's great for lunch or dinner too! Just add in some noodles, pasta, or cooked rice.

pickles
& sauces

I ONCE HEARD A CHINESE CHEF SAY, "A good pickle can save a bad dish." Now, I don't know whether that nugget of wisdom was a "Confucius says," taken from a fortune cookie or something the chef made up, but I certainly believe it. Slap some homemade Korean kimchi on a hot dog and suddenly it's gourmet. Just thinking about a really good, crunchy cucumber pickle makes me salivate. I love having a little dish of Asian pickles that I can nibble on between bites—they're refreshing and cleanse your palate.

If cooking sauces are the basis of French cooking, then dipping and chile sauces are the highlights of Asian cooking! Here are the best of the best, the most versatile sauces that go with practically anything. Dip to your heart's content!

shrimp and cucumber sunomono

Japanese cucumbers rock my world. They are slim, firm, extra crunchy, and have very few watery seeds. If you can get them, great! If not, look for long, slender English cucumbers, which are very similar, but much larger than the Japanese cucumbers. If you can't find either, don't fret! Use a regular organic cucumber, slice in half lengthwise, and use a small spoon to scoop out and discard or compost the tasteless seeds.

For a vegetarian version of this dish, substitute the shrimp with one or more of the following: julienned carrots; peeled and very thinly sliced broccoli stems, and daikon (use a vegetable peeler to get paper-thin slices); cooked, sliced, and chilled shiitake mushrooms. You can also add pickled ginger, sometimes called gari (page 30). SERVES 4

Perfect for your Sushi Temaki Party (page 100).

2 Japanese cucumbers or 1 English cucumber
1/2 teaspoon salt
1/4 pound cooked shrimp, coarsely chopped
1/2 red bell pepper, seeded and diced
1/4 teaspoon soy sauce
2 teaspoons rice vinegar (or fresh lime juice)
Pinch of sugar
1/8 teaspoon toasted sesame oil

Slice the cucumbers very thin—as thin as you can! It's best to use a mandoline to get even, paper-thin slices. Mix with the salt and let stand while you prepare the rest of the recipe.

In a bowl, combine the shrimp, bell pepper, soy sauce, rice vinegar, sugar, and sesame oil. By this time your cucumber should have released some water. Gently squeeze the cucumber to expel the moisture and discard the liquid. Mix the cucumber with the other ingredients into the bowl and serve immediately. You can make this recipe up to several hours ahead and refrigerate.

gari (pickled ginger)

I don't know who came up with adding pink coloring to pickled ginger, but I just find it unnatural. I think it has something to do with making the mound of ginger look like a flower on the plate. Pickled ginger is best in its natural color— a creamy, delicate shade. These are perfect for your Sushi Temaki Party (page 100). MAKES 1 CUP

1/4 cup rice vinegar
2 tablepoons sake (optional)
1 tablespoon water
1 tablespoon honey
1/2 teaspoon kosher or sea salt (or 1/4 teaspoon regular table salt)
1 large piece of fresh ginger, about the size of your hand

In a microwave-safe bowl, heat the vinegar, sake, and water until hot, about 20 seconds; stir in the honey and salt to dissolve. Scrape off the skin of the ginger with a teaspoon or vegetable peeler. Slice the ginger as thinly as possible, using a mandolin if you have one. Add the ginger to a nonreactive container with a tight lid. Pour in the vinegar mixture. Cover and refrigerate overnight or for at least 1 hour.

You can add beet juice if you must have it pink!

vietnamese carrot and daikon pickle

Everyone loves these pick-les. They're crunchy, sweet, tangy and go with every-thing, especially in salads and sandwiches. A forkful is a perfect addition to your avocado, tomato, and sprouts sandwich. Or emulate what dozens of hip Asian inspired food trucks do, add this pickle to hot dogs, tacos, and subs. Serve it with Vietnamese Sum-mer Rolls with Roast Pork (page 89). **MAKES 1½ CUPS**

1 cup julienned carrot
1 cup julienned daikon
Generous pinch of salt
1 tablespoon sugar
1/3 cup rice vinegar (or cider or white vinegar)

In a bowl, toss together all of the ingredients. Let sit at room temperature for 30 minutes for best flavor or refrigerate and store for up to 1 week.

korean bean sprout salad

This salad is more like a condiment. I prefer using the larger mung bean sprouts, which have a nuttier flavor, but are a little more difficult to find outside of Asian markets. You can substitute regular bean sprouts, which are available in most grocery stores. This salad is perfect for your Vegetarian Korean BBQ (page 104). SERVES 4

6 ounces mung bean sprouts
1/2 teaspoon toasted sesame oil
2 teaspoons soy sauce
2 teaspoons rice vinegar
Pinch of sugar
1 tablespoon toasted sesame seeds
Korean red pepper paste, preferably Gochujang (optional)

Bring a small pot of water to a boil. Add the bean sprouts and cook for 2 minutes. Immediately drain and rinse with cool water. In a bowl, whisk together the remaining ingredients and toss with the bean sprouts. Taste and adjust seasoning with additional soy sauce or vinegar, if needed.

quick kimchi

When I first decided to make kimchi, I consulted a very old Korean cookbook in my collection. I quickly abandoned any further attempts when the recipe instructed me to dig a hole in my yard to bury the jar of cabbage for a month. Instead of going to those extremes, I now prefer to make quick kimchi in the refrigerator. No digging required. MAKES 2 QUARTS

1 head napa cabbage
4 tablespoons kosher or sea salt (or 2 tablespoons table salt)
2 green onions, chopped
2 cloves garlic, minced
1 teaspoon grated fresh ginger
2 tablespoons hot chile paste like sambal olek (or Korean chili powder)
1/2 cup rice vinegar
2 teaspoons sugar

Remove and discard the outer leaves and the tough inner core of the napa cabbage. Shred the cabbage using a sharp chef's knife (do not use a grater).

In a large bowl, toss the shredded cabbage with the salt. Let sit at room temperature for 15 minutes. Squeeze the water from the cabbage and discard the water.

In a bowl, toss the cabbage with the remaining ingredients. Transfer to a large mason jar and refrigerate. You can eat the kimchi right away, but the flavor really develops overnight. Keep refrigerated for up to 1 month.

soy sauce kimchi

This is another refrigerator kimchi—and a milder kimchi for the spice shy. Use as much or as little chili powder as you want. Both this and the Cucumber-Apple Kimchi are perfect for your Vegetarian Korean BBQ (page 104). MAKES 1 QUART

½ head napa cabbage
1 (6-inch) piece of daikon, peeled
1 clove garlic, finely minced
1 teaspoon Korean or Asian chili powder or cayenne powder
1 cup low-sodium soy sauce
1 cup water
2 tablespoons sugar

Remove and discard the outer leaves and the tough inner core of the cabbage. Shred the cabbage using a sharp chef's knife or mandoline (do not use a grater, the cabbage will turn mushy). Thinly slice the daikon using a sharp chef's knife or mandoline.

In a large bowl, toss all of the ingredients together. Let stand for 3 hours before serving or transfer to a mason jar and refrigerate for up to 1 month.

cucumber-apple kimchi

You normally don't see apples or pears in American pickles, but their irresistible crunch makes them a natural in Asian pickles. Served chilled, they provide a refreshing way to cool your mouth after a fire-y bite of Korean BBQ. **MAKES 1 QUART**

2 Japanese cucumbers or 1 English cucumber, cut into 1/4-inch-thick sticks

1 apple (I prefer Fuji or Granny Smith) or Asian pear, peeled and cut into 1/4-inch-thick sticks

4 radishes, cut 1/8-inch-thick slices

1 fresh chile, seeded and very finely minced

Zest of 1/2 lemon

1 cup water

1 tablespoon sugar

1 teaspoon salt

1 tablespoon rice vinegar

In a large bowl, toss all of the ingredients together. Cover and refrigerate 1 hour. Serve chilled.

dumpling dipping sauce

This is my go-to sauce for dumplings. This dipping sauce is great for any type of dumplings, whether steamed, pan fried, or boiled. MAKES ¼ CUP

¼ cup low-sodium soy sauce
1 tablespoon rice vinegar (or cider vinegar)
1 teaspoon sugar
½ teaspoon very finely minced garlic
Asian chili-garlic sauce (or My Sriracha Sauce, page 42)

In a small bowl, whisk together all the ingredients. Serve immediately, or store, refrigerated, for up to 5 days.

vietnamese summer roll dipping sauce

The ultimate in salty, sweet, sour, spicy, and savory, this sauce is certain to add major flavor to anything you dip into it! Use it with Vietnamese Summer Rolls with Roast Pork (page 89) or Grilled Tofu (page 91).
MAKES ½ CUP

3½ tablespoons sugar
¾ cup hot water
3 tablespoons freshly squeezed lime juice
2 cloves garlic, finely minced
4 tablespoons fish sauce
½ teaspoon chopped fresh chile of your choice
  (or more)

In a bowl, whisk together the sugar and the water until the sugar has dissolved. Stir in the remaining ingredients. Serve immediately, or store, refrigerated, for up to 5 days.

sweet plum dipping sauce

Sweet plum sauce is a kid and crowd favorite at Chinese restaurants—it's a pretty orangey-peach color and so sweet. Serve with Vietnamese Summer Rolls with Roast Pork (page ~~89~~) or Grilled Tofu (page 91).

MAKES ¼ CUP

¼ cup sweet plum sauce (sometimes called "duck sauce")

½ teaspoon fish sauce

½ teaspoon grated fresh ginger

In a bowl, stir together the ingredients. Serve immediately, or store, refrigerated, for up to 5 days.

ponzu sauce

Ponzu is a Japanese citrusy soy sauce, awesome for dipping or drizzling. You can't go wrong with any fresh citrus, choose your favorite. We used to have a calamansi lime tree, the fruit grew like crazy and were the size of a jumbo marble. Every day, I'd go out and pick the limes for ponzu, mojitos. Five of them would easily fit in my pocket. One day I forgot I had them in my back pocket and sat down. Smush.

Perfect for use in Blackened Tofu with Ginger Ponzu Sauce (pate 112).

MAKES ⅔ CUP

⅓ cup soy sauce
¼ cup dashi (page 14) or vegetable stock (page 11)
3 tablespoons freshly squeezed lemon, orange, or lime juice
½ teaspoon sugar

Whisk together all ingredients. You can keep ponzu sauce in the refrigerator for up to 2 weeks.

my sriracha sauce

When I was in elementary school, a businessman asked my dad to invest in a local company called Huy Fong. Apparently they needed additional capital to grow the company. Unfortunately my Dad declined. Huy Fong is the maker of the very famous, red bottle, green cap "rooster" sriracha hot sauce that sits on nearly every Vietnamese, Thai, and Chinese restaurant table. That sound you just heard? That was me smacking my Dad's forehead for not investing.

I'm a big fan of sriracha sauce, and lately I've outgrown the rooster brand and instead either make my own or buy my latest obsession, "Yuzu Pao" sriracha sauce made with chiles and a little bit of yuzu citrus.

Be careful when chopping hot chiles. Use gloves or cover your hand with a plastic sandwich bag. The color of your sriracha sauce depends on the colors of your chiles. I've used mostly red chiles and it turns a gorgeous sunset orange.

Perfect for any recipe, especially Mapo Tofu (page 158). **MAKES 1½ CUPS**

Tastes infinitely better than the rooster!

2 teaspoons cooking oil

¼ pound fresh chiles from the hot list (see page 43), chopped

¼ pound fresh chiles from the mild list (see page 43), chopped

4 cloves garlic, chopped

2 tablespoons light brown sugar or palm sugar

4 tablespoons rice vinegar or white vinegar

1 tablespoon fish sauce

½ cup water

Heat the oil in frying pan over medium heat. When hot, add the chile and garlic. Turn the heat to medium-low and cook for 7 to 10 minutes, stirring occasionally. Be careful not to burn the peppers or garlic.

Stir in the remaining ingredients and adjust seasoning according to taste. Transfer to a blender, cover and purée until smooth. Store in the refrigerator for up to 2 weeks.

HOT CHILES:
Cayenne
Cherry
Fresno
Habanero
Holland or Dutch
Jalapeño
Serrano
Thai Chile

MILDER CHILES:
Anaheim
Banana (also known as Hungarian wax)
Pasilla
Shishito
Sweet peppers

salads & dressings

THE SECRET TO A SUCCESSFUL SALAD is the element of surprise—nothing makes me happier than someone saying, "Wow, I love that crunchy bit in the salad!" or "What's in this dressing!?" Because, let's face it, these days it's so easy to make a lazy, boring salad: just rip open a bag and glug some bottled dressing on.

Keep it creative enough, and salad can even be the star of the meal. I love making my own salad dressings; it's simple and so much healthier than anything you can find in the store. Most Western salad dressings are too oily, thick, and fatty for my taste. Asian-style dressings are light and zippy, with minimal amounts of oil. Salads ingredients should be lightly flavored with dressing, not dripping or coated.

When making dressings, I like using mild or neutral flavored oil, like rice bran oil, grapeseed oil, or light vegetable oil. If you're using olive oil, use a light olive oil, otherwise it can be too strong in flavor.

Feel free to mix and match the dressings with any of the salads!

orange-soy vinaigrette

1 clove garlic, finely minced
2 1/2 tablespoons low-sodium
  soy sauce
1 teaspoon sesame oil
2 1/2 tablespoons rice vinegar
1/2 orange, zested and juiced

Add all ingredients to a mason jar, close lid tightly, and shake a few times.

sesame-ponzu vinaigrette

1 tablespoon ponzu sauce
  (page 41)
1 teaspoon sesame seeds
1 tablespoon chopped green
  onions
1/2 teaspoon toasted sesame oil

Add all ingredients to a mason jar, close lid tightly, and shake a few times.

peanut dressing & dipping sauce

1 clove garlic, finely minced
3 tablespoons hot water
1/2 cup peanut butter
1 tablespoon brown sugar
Juice of 1 lime
2 tablespoons soy sauce

Add all ingredients to a mason jar, close lid tightly, and shake a few times.

orange-sesame dressing

1 1/2 tablespoons finely grated
carrot (use microplane grater)
1 teaspoon finely grated fresh
ginger
1 tablespoon miso paste
1 tablespoon rice vinegar
1/2 teaspoon toasted sesame oil
1/4 cup water
1 teaspoon sesame seeds

Add all ingredients to a mason jar, close lid tightly, and shake a few times.

asian slaw with wasabi-soy dressing

Imagine a slaw that's bright, crunchy, and fresh, instead of drowning and dripping in mayonnaise. I've never understood the mayonnaise obsession with coleslaws—it's too thick, heavy, and renders the vegetables tasteless! Instead, I like tossing lots of crunchy, fresh vegetables like cabbage, jicama, bell pepper, and cucumber with a vinaigrette. Serve with burgers or enjoy it as a salad in itself. SERVES 4

1 small jicama, peeled and julienned
1 bell pepper, seeded and julienned
1 cucumber, julienned
¼ purple cabbage, shredded
Wasabi-Soy Dressing (page 51)

Toss the slaw ingredients with the dressing, and serve.

Lots of crunchy vegetables makes a great slaw!

gado gado

This is a mixed salad from Indonesia with a peanutty dressing. It's a one-bowl meal, especially if you make a BIG bowl! In addition to the raw vegetables found in a most salads, I like to add several cooked ingredients: a hard-boiled egg, blanched green beans, and cooked noodles. You can also add fried tofu, boiled potatoes, or tempeh (my girlfriend Kelly's favorite ingredient).

SERVES 4

Fun to say and fun to eat!

¼ pound green beans, ends trimmed
8 ounces noodles of your choice
2 eggs
1 large tomato, cut into thin wedges
¼ cucumber, julienned
1 handful of lettuce, shredded
1 handful of bean sprouts
Peanut Dressing (page 49)

Bring a large pot of water to a boil. Add the green beans and cook for 3 to 4 minutes until crisp-tender. Use tongs and a sieve to remove the green beans, drain, and set aside. Return the same water to a boil and cook the noodles according to package instructions. Use tongs and a sieve to drain and remove the noodles and set aside.

Turn off the heat and carefully slide in the eggs. Cover the pot and let sit for 8 to 10 minutes. Remove the eggs (do not peel) and, with a very sharp chef's knife, cut each egg in half lengthwise. Use a spoon to scoop out the egg from each half and discard shell. Assemble the salad, toss with the dressing, and serve.

edamame noodle salad

Don't talk to me when I'm eating this noodle salad. My friend Kelly made this mistake the first time we made it and in an attempt to slurp up the slippery noodles and answer her by nodding "yes," I whipped myself in the eye with a stray noodle. So please, leave the convo for later. Freshly squeezed orange juice (just half an orange is all it takes) and the powerful zest combined with soy sauce is the base of this dressing. Use whatever noodles call out to you, even angel hair pasta. SERVES 4

6 ounces dried noodles
1/2 pint cherry tomatoes, quartered
8 ounces shelled, cooked edamame
1 green onion, chopped
Orange-Soy Vinaigrette (page 48)

Bring a pot of water to boil and cook the noodles according to the package instructions. Drain the noodles and rinse with cool water. In a large bowl, combine the noodles, tomatoes, edamame, and green onions. Toss with the vinaigrette and serve.

Slurptastic!

seared scallop salad with sesame-ginger vinaigrette

You know what makes me happy? Big, fat, meaty scallops. Sometimes for lunch, if there's nothing that appeals to me, I grab a bag of frozen scallops, defrost a handful, and pan fry 'em to throw on a salad. Keep a bag of these frozen jewels in the freezer (they're frozen at sea). They defrost in minutes and you can cook as many as you like. Just don't overcook them or they'll be rubbery. SERVES 4

16 large scallops
Salt and freshly ground pepper
2 teaspoons cooking oil
4 large handfuls of salad greens
Sesame-Ginger Vinaigrette (page 47)

Season the scallops with salt and pepper on both sides. Heat a frying pan over high heat. When hot, swirl in the oil. Add the scallops in a single layer to the pan (you might have to cook in two batches). Let cook, undisturbed, for 2 minutes. Flip the scallops and cook another 2 minutes. Turn the heat to medium and cook for 2 minutes longer.

Assemble the salad greens and scallops, drizzle with dressing, and serve.

HERE'S A TIP: *Buy scallops that are "dry packed" and not floating in milky liquid, which means they've been sitting in preservatives. Dry-packed scallops should look firm and slightly wet.*

little bites

APPETIZERS, OR WHAT I CALL, "LITTLE BITES," set the tone for dinner parties. It's a little tease, something to turn on the taste buds and tummy while the rest of the meal is prepared. At my house, I have Little Bites on the kitchen counter, and guests in the kitchen—whoever is helping me—get first dibs. Our private little "cooks nibbles."

korean beef bites

Tender steak is seasoned in traditional Korean BBQ bulgogi marinade, sliced thin, and set atop a rice cracker with a healthy dose of fiery kimchi on top. If you're having a party, I would advise you to double this recipe—yeah, it's that good. MAKES 24

Betcha can't eat just one.

1/2 pound flank or sirloin steak
1 tablespoon low-sodium soy sauce or gluten-free tamari
1 teaspoon brown sugar
1/2 teaspoon sesame oil
1 clove garlic, finely minced
1/2 teaspoon freshly grated ginger
24 rice crackers
1/2 cup prepared kimchi
1 green onion, very thinly sliced on the diagonal

Slice the steak as thin as you can into at least 24 pieces. If you are using flank steak, make sure to slice across the grain. In a large bowl, whisk together the soy sauce, brown sugar, sesame oil, garlic, and ginger. Add the steak and mix to coat. Marinate for at least 10 minutes at room temperature or up to 24 hours in the refrigerator.

Heat a grill pan over high heat. You'll cook the steak in batches to avoid overcrowding the pan. When the pan is hot, add the steak, and grill 1 to 2 minutes per side, depending on the thickness of your slices.

To serve, on each rice cracker layer a slice of steak, the kimchi, and garnish with green onion.

crispy rice patties

OK, these are a little tricky to make, meaning you must follow the directions. Don't go off-script! But what a fab way to use up any rice left in the pot. You must use same-day cooked rice (not leftover rice that has been refrigerated) so that the patties stick together. These patties are crispy, crunchy, and puffy! A dab of soy sauce is brushed on top before the patties go on the skillet.

¼ cup cooked rice per patty
Cooking oil
Soy sauce

Line a baking sheet with parchment or wax paper. Fill a bowl with cool water.

Dip your hands in the water, shaking off the excess (this prevents the rice from sticking to your hands). Scoop up a small handful of rice (about the size of a golf ball). Shape into a flat patty. Place the patty on the prepared baking sheet. Repeat with the remaining rice. You'll need to dip your hands in the water for each patty. Chill in the refrigerator for at least 1 hour or up to eight hours.

Heat a nonstick skillet on medium heat. When hot, swirl in the oil. Brush both sides of the rice patty with soy sauce. Add as many rice patties as will fit in the skillet. Cook for 3 to 4 minutes per side, or until crispy. Serve immediately.

Best. Snack. Ever.

seared ahi tuna

I once chatted with a successful restaurateur who told me that his seared ahi tuna was the most popular appetizer across all of his properties. And not a single one of the restaurants was Asian. So I think it's safe to say that seared ahi tuna has crossed over from a traditional Japanese dish into the mainstream.

All the tuna needs is a quick dusting of salt, pepper, and ground coriander and then sear it in a very hot pan. I like it served simply with wasabi and soy sauce and a side of pickled ginger (page 30). One rule and one rule only: Do not overcook the tuna. **SERVES** 4

1 pound very fresh ahi tuna fillet
⅛ teaspoon ground coriander
Salt and freshly ground black pepper
2 teaspoons cooking oil

CONDIMENTS
Low-sodium soy sauce with a drop of sesame oil
Prepared wasabi
2 tablespoons finely sliced green onion
Prepared pickled ginger (page 30)

Season the tuna on both sides with coriander, salt, and pepper. Heat a frying pan on high. When hot, swirl in the oil. Sear the tuna, 3 minutes per side and remove from heat. Slice into 1½ inch pieces and serve with the condiments.

thai larb chicken lettuce cups

Larb is an Asian salad that's considered the national dish of Laos. It features a sour and spicy warm stir-fried meat on top of cold, crisp lettuce. The dressing is made of fish sauce, spicy fresh chiles, and fresh lime juice. Fresh mint leaves provide a refreshing finish.

On the list of my favorite sounds would be the crisp snap crunch of supercold lettuce as you peel off the layers, one by one. Use iceberg, Boston bibb, or any kind of lettuce that has cup-shaped leaves for this recipe. Keep the lettuce refrigerated until ready to eat. SERVES 4

1 1/2 tablespoons cooking oil
1/2 pound ground chicken breast
2 shallots, diced
1/4 red onion, diced
1 clove garlic, very finely minced
Minced fresh chiles, Jalapeño or Fresno (amount up to you)
1 tablespoon fish sauce
1/2 lime, juiced
1 teaspoon low-sodium soy sauce
1 head iceberg lettuce, leaves separated into "cups"
1 handful of cilantro and/or mint, cut into chiffonade

Heat a wok or large sauté pan over high heat. When hot, swirl in 1 tablespoon of the oil and add the chicken. Use your spatula to break up the meat and spread out over the surface of the pan. Cook until browned, about 3 minutes.

Push the ground chicken to one side of the pan and swirl in the remaining 1/2 tablespoon of oil. To the oil, add the shallots, red onion, garlic, and fresh chiles and sauté the aromatics until fragrant, about 30 seconds. Add the fish sauce, lime juice, and soy sauce.

Serve with lettuce cups and herbs.

vietnamese-style shrimp cocktail

The first time I ever had shrimp cocktail, I was seven years old and our family got dressed up to go out to dinner at the fanciest restaurant in town. Back then, we lived in the small town of North Platte, Nebraska, and the fancy schmancy place to eat was actually the airport restaurant! I wanted the shrimp cocktail so badly, but I knew it was expensive. My parents let me order it anyway, even if they didn't care for it. I felt like a rich society girl, holding each shrimp by the tail with my pinky up. In all honesty, I don't think I even liked the taste (bland boiled shrimp dipped in cold ketchupy sauce?), but I had to pretend to like it at $7.99 for five shrimp!

This Asianified version uses Clamato (savory tomato juice), fish sauce, garlic, fresh chiles, and avocado; it's everything a shrimp appetizer at a fancy restaurant should be—fresh, vibrant, and tingly spicy. SERVES 4

DRESSING
1 teaspoon fish sauce
1 clove garlic, very finely minced
1/2 teaspoon very finely minced hot chile (jalapeño, Thai, serrano)
1/2 lime, juiced
Pinch of sugar
1/2 teaspoon hot chili sauce, such as My Sriracha Sauce (page 42)

1 tomato, diced
1 stalk celery, diced
1/2 bell pepper, diced
1/2 avocado, diced
1/4 pound cooked small salad shrimp
8 ounces tomato juice or Clamato
1 tablespoon finely minced cilantro

In a large bowl, whisk together the dressing ingredients. Toss in the remaining ingredients and chill in the refrigerator for 30 minutes. Serve cold.

crab-mango salad

Last year I was informed that I have been mispronouncing "endive." I was at a food conference and the Belgian endive association reps were at a booth handing out perfect pale leaves filled with seafood salad. I was scolded by the booth leader, "No, no, you must say it like me: 'OHN-deeve.'" I guess their marketing people thought they needed to promote a high-class image of endive, otherwise known as "white gold."

Well, either way you pronounce it (I'm sticking with my American "EN-dive"), it makes for great finger food. SERVES 4 TO 6

DRESSING
2 tablespoons fruity olive oil
2 tablespoons rice vinegar
2 teaspoons fish sauce or low-sodium soy sauce
2 tablespoons water

1 cup cooked crabmeat
1 mango, diced
1 green onion, green part only, finely minced
Minced fresh chile of your choice, to taste
2 heads Belgian endive, leaves separated

In a small bowl, whisk together the dressing ingredients.

In a bowl, gently mix the crabmeat with the mango, green onion, and chile. Toss in the dressing.

To serve, spoon some of the crab mixture onto each endive leaf.

chicken-tofu pot stickers

We Asians love our dumplings! Guo tie (Chinese), gyoza (Japanese), and mandu (Korean)—each culture has its own name for pan-fried dumplings and also its own ingredients. I've lightened up the normal pot sticker recipe, subbing lean ground chicken for the fatty pork typically used. Salt is used to expel water from the vegetables—don't worry about the amount of salt in the ingredients, most of it will be discarded in the water.

MAKES 50 POT STICKERS

1/2 small head cabbage (about 12 ounces)
1 carrot, peeled
3/4 teaspoon salt
1 pound ground chicken
7 ounces soft or silken tofu
2 teaspoons soy sauce
1 teaspoon sesame oil
1 clove garlic, finely minced
1 teaspoon freshly grated ginger
1/4 teaspoon freshly ground pepper
1 tablespoon cornstarch
1/2 cup cool water
1 package of 50 round pot sticker wrappers, about 3 1/2-inch diameter
Cooking oil
Andrew's Secret Sauce (page 36), Pow Pow Sauce (page 120), Scallion Dipping Sauce (page 31), Dumpling Dipping Sauce (page 38), or My Sriracha Sauce (page 42)

Grate the cabbage and carrot on the large holes of a box grater. In a large bowl, combine the cabbage and carrot with the salt. Set aside for 15 minutes. Grab a handful of the vegetables at a time and squeeze hard to expel the water and discard.

Return the vegetables to the bowl and mix in the ground chicken, tofu, soy sauce, sesame oil, garlic, ginger, and pepper. Use a large wooden spoon to mix and break up the tofu into pea-sized pieces.

continued

chicken-tofu pot stickers, continued

HERE'S A TIP: *For defrosting dumpling wrappers, place them in the refrigerator overnight, on the counter for 1 hour, or in the microwave on the defrost setting for 2 minutes. Do not submerge the package in water!*

In a small bowl, mix together the cornstarch and water. Set aside. Spoon a heaping teaspoon of the filling in the middle of a pot sticker wrapper. Dip a finger into the cornstarch slurry and paint the edge of the wrapper, all the way around. Fold the wrapper over like a half-moon and press tightly to make a seal. Arrange the folded pot stickers in a single layer (not touching) on a plate or baking sheet. Cover with a barely-damp towel or plastic wrap to prevent drying.

When ready to cook, heat a large frying pan over medium heat. Swirl in 1½ teaspoons of cooking oil. Arrange pot stickers in a single layer in the pan. Try not to crowd or they'll stick to each other. Cook until slightly browned, about 1 minute, then flip and brown the other side, about 1 minute longer. Carefully pour in 2 tablespoons water, using the pan lid to protect you from the spattering. Cover and cook until water has evaporated and the dumplings are cooked through, about 3 minutes. Repeat with the remaining pot stickers, wiping the pan clean between batches. Serve immediately with dipping sauce.

shrimp and spinach dumplings

Hurray for healthy dumplings! If you're looking for a super-fast, super-easy, and nearly fat-free dumpling, this is it. Minced fresh shrimp and chopped spinach are wrapped into a dumpling and boiled in either water or vegetable stock.

Dumplings can go straight from freezer to stove top! Lay uncooked dumplings on a paper plate in a single layer. Slide entire plate into a gallon-sized freezer bag, seal and freeze for another day. When ready to cook, drop frozen dumplings into boiling water and cook for 12 minutes. MAKES 35 DUMPLINGS

Make an extra batch to freeze for a lazy day!

2 teaspoons cornstarch

2 tablespoons cool water

1 (10-ounce) box frozen chopped spinach, defrosted

1 pound shrimp, shelled and minced

1 teaspoon grated fresh ginger

2 teaspoons minced fresh basil

2 teaspoons light soy sauce

1 teaspoon toasted sesame oil

1 1/2 teaspoons rice vinegar

1 package of 50 frozen dumpling wrappers (about 3 1/2-inch diameter), defrosted (see tip for defrosting wrappers on page 78)

2 quarts vegetable stock (optional, page 11)

Andrew's Secret Sauce (page 36), Pow Pow Sauce (page 120), Scallion Dipping Sauce (page 31), Dumpling Dipping Sauce (page 38), or My Sriracha Sauce (page 42)

continued

shrimp and spinach
dumplings, continued

In a small bowl combine 1 teaspoon of the cornstarch and the water. Set aside. Using your hands, squeeze out as much water as possible from the spinach. Place the dry spinach into a large bowl (discard the spinach water or save it for making stock).

Add shrimp, ginger, basil, soy sauce, sesame oil, rice vinegar, and the remaining 1 teaspoon cornstarch to the bowl with the spinach and mix well.

Spoon a heaping teaspon of the filling in the middle of each wrapper. Fold the dumpling over like a half-moon, sealing the edge with the reserved cornstarch mixture. Arrange the dumplings in a single layer (not touching) on a plate or baking sheet. Cover with a barely-damp towel or plastic wrap to prevent drying.

Boil a large pot of stock or water. Cook the dumplings in batches. Carefully slide about one-third of the dumplings into the water and cook for 6 to 8 minutes. Drain and repeat with remaining dumplings. Serve immediately with your choice of sauces.

roasted chestnuts

As a little girl in Hong Kong, I would go to the open-air markets with my Gong Gong (grandpa). Near his clothing shop there were a few roasted chestnut street vendors. They'd sing out "Roasted Chestnuts! Roasted Chestnuts!" and I'd always ask Gong Gong for coins to buy a bag. Sometimes they'd be handed to me in a newspaper cone, sometimes in a thin, brown paper bag folded over. Gong Gong would tell me to put the bag in my pocket to keep my hands warm.

SERVES 6 AS A SNACK

2 pounds chestnuts

Soak the chestnuts in water for 1 hour (optional, but it makes the chestnuts easier to open).

Heat the oven to oven to 425°F. With your paring knife, cut an X-shaped slit on the flat side of the chestnut. Place chestnuts on a baking sheet and roast for 20 minutes. Peel chestnuts while they are still hot, using a towel to hold them. (As the chestnuts cool, the shell will harden and make them difficult to peel.)

If a raw chestnut feels light, drop it in a bowl of water. If the chestnut floats, it's no good to eat and probably rotten inside. Just discard.

Try chestnuts raw. They're crunchy, sweet, and mild!

chicken-mango lettuce cups

Seven months out of the year, we have a nice variety of lettuce growing in our garden, the remaining five months in Southwest Florida are just too hot for the delicate leaves. The first time I shopped for seeds online, I was inundated with choices and we ended up with so many varieties of lettuce—Red Fire, Red Sails, Lobjoits, Cimmaron— that I started serving every meal with lettuce cups.

I want you to experiment with this recipe! Use whatever vegetables or meats your family loves. Only one rule: eat with your hands! SERVES 4 AS A MAIN DISH OR 8 AS AN APPETIZER

1 pound ground chicken
2 teaspoons soy sauce
1 teaspoon cornstarch, potato starch, or rice starch
1 teaspoon cooking oil
1 green onion, chopped
6 ounces fresh shiitake mushrooms, sliced
2 teaspoons seasoned rice vinegar
1/2 teaspoon toasted sesame oil
1 large mango, diced
1 head lettuce, leaves separated

In a large bowl, mix the chicken with the soy sauce and cornstarch.

Heat a wok or large sauté pan over medium heat. When hot, swirl in the oil. Stir-fry the green onion and shiitake mushrooms for 1 minute. Turn the heat to high and add the chicken. Stir-fry until cooked through, 5 to 7 minutes. Stir in the rice vinegar, sesame oil, and mango. Remove from the heat and serve with the lettuce cups.

EXPERIMENT WITH THESE OTHER INGREDIENTS: *bell pepper (diced) • edamame beans • fresh bean sprouts (as a topping for crunch) • frozen peas (stir in frozen during last 2 minutes of cooking) • ground turkey • beef • lamb • pork • hot chili sauce (1 teaspoon stirred in) • mandarin oranges (as a topping) • onions (chopped) • shrimp or scallops (coarsely chop before marinating) • spinach leaves (stir in to wilt) • zucchini (diced)*

grilled shishito peppers

I grow a lot of Asian vegetables in my garden. Some of them are the standards, like bok choy and Chinese broccoli (gai lan) and a handful are my special plants, which get the best soil, best location for maximum sun, and extra compost. One of these plants is the Japanese shishito pepper: green, wrinkly, thin-skinned, and very sweet. I like to grill or broil shishito; the skin blisters like crepe paper and you eat the entire thing. They are similar to Spanish padrón peppers, which you can substitute in this recipe. This recipe gives three different methods for cooking the peppers. SERVES 6 AS A SNACK

1 pound fresh shishito peppers
Cooking oil
Good sea salt

ON THE GRILL: Preheat the grill to medium-high. Thread a few shishito peppers onto a bamboo skewer.

Lightly brush or drizzle with oil. Grill for 3 minutes, flip and grill 3 to 4 minutes longer, until the pepper begins to blister. Season with sea salt. Serve.

IN THE OVEN: Preheat the broiler and position the rack 6 inches from the heat source. Place peppers on a baking sheet and coat lightly with oil. Broil 3 to 4 minutes each side.

ON THE STOVE: No need to skewer, add a little cooking oil to a frying pan over medium heat. Add the peppers and cook for 4 minutes. Shake the pan to flip the peppers and cook until browned all over. Salt to taste and serve hot.

share

WE HAVE GUESTS OVER FOR DINNER EVERY WEEK. My house has become the gathering place for my friends to unwind from the workweek and have a glass of wine, or two, or three. Our dinner parties are not fancy, there are no ties or high heels. Instead, my good friends show up in flip-flops, shorts, and swim suits. Our Florida weather gives us pool-worthy and outdoor grilling weather nine-tenths of the year. (The one-tenth of time we stay inside is hurricane season!)

Most of my friends have little kids, and they know exactly how to make themselves at home. Kick off shoes, yank on boots (at last count, we have nineteen pairs of boots in all different sizes for our guests), pet the chickens, check for any eggs, pick green beans, and pluck salad leaves from the garden, and when that's all done, run straight into the pool.

I love planning meals that involve everyone cooking their own food—from Korean BBQ with a tabletop grill to sushi parties where you make your own hand rolls. The sharing aspect of food is cooking together *and* eating together. It's fun, social, and interactive. In fact, I read in a trends report online that "social cooking and eating" is the next big thing (but hey, you read it here first, right!?)—with dinner parties featuring fondues and raclettes becoming all the rage.

vietnamese summer rolls with roast pork

Once a year, my girlfriends Ree Drummond (www.the pioneerwoman.com), Elise Bauer (www.simplyrecipes .com), and I host a massive party for hundreds of food bloggers. If creating a recipe for 500 hungry food bloggers isn't pressure, I don't know what is! This recipe, featuring pork roast cooked in a slow cooker, was served one year. If you're hosting a party, this is such an easy recipe. Let the pork roast cook in the slow cooker and then thinly slice. Lay out all of the vegetables on the table, along with fresh herbs, rice paper, and dipping sauce. Everyone can roll their own summer rolls, even the kids! SERVES 4

ROAST PORK

2 pounds boneless pork roast
Salt and freshly ground black pepper
1 teaspoon ground coriander
1 cup freshly squeezed orange juice
1 cup chicken stock (page 10)
2 tablespoons fish sauce
6 cloves garlic, smashed
2 teaspoons chopped fresh ginger
1 onion, cut into 1/4-inch-thick slices
1 orange, cut into 1/4-inch-thick slices (skin on)

SUMMER ROLLS

1 carrot, julienned
1 cucumber, julienned
1 bell pepper, seeded and julienned
4 ounces baby spinach leaves
10 mint sprigs
10 basil sprigs
1 to 2 (12-ounce) packages rice paper spring roll wrappers
Sweet Plum Dipping Sauce (page 40)

Season the pork on all sides with salt, pepper, and coriander. To a slow cooker, add the orange juice, chicken stock, fish sauce, garlic, and ginger. Layer half of the sliced onions and sliced oranges in the cooker. Place pork on top. Cover with remaining sliced onions and oranges. Cook for 4 to 5 hours.

Remove pork from slow cooker, let cool for 15 minutes. Slice the pork as thin as you can.

continued

A slow cooker recipe!

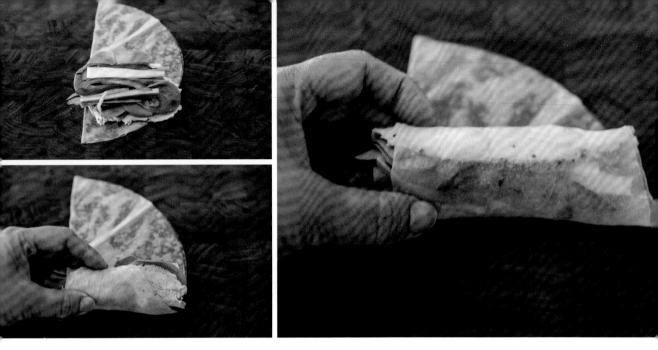

vietnamese summer rolls with roast pork, continued

To make the rolls, make sure all of your ingredients are prepared. Fill a pie plate or large bowl with hot water (about bath temperature).

Dip each rice paper wrapper in the hot water for 2 seconds per side. Let excess water drip off.

Lay the damp rice paper on a clean, dry surface. When it begins to soften, fold the wrapper in half.

Lay a slice of roast pork on the bottom half of the roll. Layer on the vegetables and herbs.

Beginning at the bottom and keeping the roll tight, roll the filling up in the wraper. Repeat with remaining ingredients and wrappers.

Cover with plastic wrap and refrigerate until ready to serve.

Serve with the dipping sauce.

vietnamese summer rolls with grilled tofu

Diane and Todd of White on Rice Couple (www.white onricecouple.com) are like family to us! I first met Diane online, through blogging and email exchanges. Our first dinner together was at their house, I brought the kids with me and we had such a magical evening. Diane and Todd taught me how to make summer rolls, dinner party style. We dined in their backyard, surrounded by their beloved fruit trees. The long table was overflowing with herbs plucked fresh, julienned vegetables, chopped chiles, tangy dipping sauces. At the center was a portable butane burner sizzling marinated eggplant, pork, and tofu that you cooked yourself. It was a DIY summer roll party! We rolled all night long.

SERVES 4

2 teaspoons fish sauce
2 teaspoons soy sauce
1 clove garlic, finely minced
1 teaspoon grated fresh ginger
14 ounces extra-firm fresh tofu, cut into 1/2-inch strips
1 tablespoon cooking oil
1 head leafy lettuce
2 carrots, julienned
1 cucumber, julienned (English or Japanese cucumber work best)
10 basil sprigs
10 cilantro sprigs
1 (12-ounce) package rice paper spring roll wrappers
Vietnamese Summer Roll Dipping Sauce (page 39)

Combine the fish sauce, soy sauce, garlic, and ginger in a pie plate or bowl. Add the tofu and marinate for at least 15 minutes or up to overnight in the refrigerator.

Heat a nonstick frying pan over medium-high heat. Swirl in the cooking oil and when hot, carefully add the tofu. Fry 1 minute each side.

To make the rolls, make sure all of your ingredients are prepared. Fill a pie plate or large bowl with hot water (about bath temperature).

Dip each rice paper wrapper in the hot water for 2 seconds per side. Let excess water drip off.

continued

vietnamese summer
rolls with grilled tofu,
continued

Lay the damp rice paper on a clean, dry surface. When it begins to soften, fold the wrapper in half.

Position your vegetables on the bottom half of the wrapper. Top with one piece of tofu and some of the herbs.

Starting at the bottom, and keeping the roll tight, roll up the ingredients into the wrapper. Repeat with the remaining ingredients and wrappers. Serve with dipping sauce.

If you are rolling a batch to enjoy later, transfer the summer rolls to a plate in a single layer, cover with plastic wrap and refrigerate for up to 8 hours, until ready to serve. Serve with the dipping sauce.

HERE'S A TIP: *If you love eggplant, cut into pieces about the size of a potato wedge. Marinate like the tofu. Grill eggplant 1 minute on each side.*

chinese hot pot party

Chinese fondue is called "hot pot." A large, wide pot of bubbling broth sits on a portable butane burner in the middle of a round dining table (round is best, so everyone has equal access to the pot) and jam-packed around the table are palm-sized dishes of every type of seafood, vegetable, and meat you can imagine, ready to cook. All the ingredients, from fresh fish, scallops, and clams to paper-thin-sliced lamb, pork, and beef are cut into bite-sized pieces that cook in a flash, sometimes with just a 15-second swirl in the boiling broth.

I arm each person with a pair of chopsticks, a little basket for cooking, and assorted dipping sauces. The delicate wire basket has a long, skinny, twisted handle. The basket handle is malleable and bendable, which is important later on. You choose the ingredients that go into your little basket: a snap pea, a rock shrimp, and maybe a bay scallop can fit in one go. Lower the basket into the hot pot and wait anywhere from a few seconds to a couple of minutes for it to cook. If you bend the handle into a hook shape, to fit the shape of the pot's edge, your hands are free to eat the previous batch cooling on your plate. And this is where the fun begins.

As my family sits around the table, my brother Jay is the first to claim his territory in the pot. He fills his basket with meat, submerges it in the hot broth, cricks the handle, and lets it hang on the edge. That's one side. He then grabs his chopsticks, spears the scallop, and lets it cook about two inches away from the basket. The space that extends from the pie-shaped wedge right in front of him to the area in the hot pot between the basket and the chopsticks belongs him. That's his way of marking his territory.

Now, Mom, Dad, my husband Scott, and I try to do the same thing. As the last person, I have to wedge my way in to claim some little spot in the pot. It may seem like I have the least advantage, but it always turns out that

being the last is the smartest position to have. Without a basket to watch over (to ensure the meat doesn't overcook), I'm free to use nimble chopsticks and quick eyes to snag, steal, and swim for stray nuggets of food that have floated free from the baskets, especially from Scott, who always seems to overfill his basket.

The problem is, these very light baskets have no lid, and when you try to submerge the thing in wildly bubbly, boiling broth, it ends up bobbing recklessly this way and that. Which is why the crick in the handle is important to latch onto the edge, though most of the time it proves ineffective.

There's nothing more disappointing than lifting up my basket that once held a full catch, only to have it come up with barely a scrap that resembles nibbled bait, while my husband snickers in delight next to me.

The quiet and calculating game of "You snatch mine, I'll snatch yours" ensues, which quickly escalates into downright plucking of a perfectly cooked clam right from someone's chopsticks just milliseconds before it reaches their lips.

sushi temaki party
party, continued

SERVES 6

RAW SEAFOOD (CHOOSE 2 TO 3, TOTALING ¹/₂ TO 1 POUND)

Arctic char

Mahi mahi

Pacific albacore tuna

Sablefish

Yellowtail or yellowfin tuna

Cut each piece of fish into small thin strips, about the size of a fat French fry.

COOKED SEAFOOD CHOOSE 2 TO 3, TOTALING ¹/₂ TO 1 POUND)

Boiled shrimp

Broiled scallops

Cooked crabmeat

Grilled salmon

Seared tuna

Smoked salmon

VEGETABLES & FRUIT (CHOOSE 5 TO 6, TOTALING 1¹/₂ TO 2 POUNDS)

Asparagus, either roasted or steamed to crisp-tender

Avocado

Bell peppers, cut into thin strips

Carrots, julienned

Cucumber, julienned

Fresh herbs like cilantro, parsley, basil, mint, chives, shiso, dill

Green beans, either roasted or steamed to crisp-tender

Green onion, finely minced

Japanese pickles

Kiwi, thinly sliced

Leafy lettuce, leaves only, no tough stems

Mango, thinly sliced

Mushrooms, sautéed in a little butter

Spinach, blanched and squeezed dry

Sprouts

Tomatoes, diced

Low-sodium soy sauce

Pickled ginger (page 30)

Seasoned rice vinegar

Seaweed, sheets cut in half to measure about 4 by 10 inches.

Sushi rice or short-grain rice

sushi temaki party

With the way my friends and I love sushi, we would go broke if it weren't for our at-home sushi parties. Instead of a thick glass shield and a counter between you and the fish, each person is their own master sushi chef at these parties.

A dining table is filled with small plates of ingredients: thinly sliced hamachi, minced tuna with green onions and chili oil, broiled sea scallops with miso butter, sharp spears of asparagus, little orbs of salty caviar, creamy avocado slices, crunchy matchstick carrots or sweet mango, just to name a few possibilities.

The first step is to get a piece of seaweed on your plate, then add a little rice as your base. Walk around the table and examine the different sushi combination possibilities. Fill your own hand roll with whatever your tummy desires. You could be like my friend Wendy, who loves to make a different veggie roll every time or you could be like her husband, Shawn, who loves to keep it simple with seaweed, rice and raw fish—no frilly extras.

For those who love raw fish, check out my friend Martin's company, I Love Blue Sea (www.ilovebluesea.com). They sell only fresh, safe, and sustainable sushi-grade fish: Pacific albacore tuna, arctic char, Hawaiian yellowtail, and black cod. They offer flat rate overnight shipping and the best part is that you know you're a responsible sushi-lovin' person. Also, be sure to get real wasabi; check out chefshop.com. Most sushi places serve fake wasabi made from food coloring and horseradish. Real wasabi is milder, smooth, fresh, and the kick is more like a slow heat than a sharp bite.

Here's what you'll need for your sushi party:

continued

Make sure all ingredients are cut into bite-sized pieces. Meats should be sliced as thinly as possible. Each person should have a medium-size bowl and a couple of dipping-sauce trays.

Position the portable stove in the middle of the table. Place large pot on the stove and fill with the 1½ quarts of vegetable stock. Add another quart of water and bring to a boil. When simmering, turn the heat to low.

Start by throwing in a bunch of vegetables; they'll cook throughout the meal and you can replenish as you eat. Have each person take a couple of morsels for their basket and cook in the stock: beef is generally ready in 30 seconds, chicken and pork take a little longer. Remove the basket from the stock when you think the food is cooked, dip morsels in sauce, and enjoy. A few times during the meal, you may have to replenish the stock in the pot with the water-vegetable stock mixture.

Toward the end of the meal, the stock has become flavorful and rich and everyone is ready to enjoy some of it. Swirl all of the cooked noodles in and serve.

chinese hot pot party, continued

SERVES 6

SEAFOOD & MEATS (CHOOSE 2 TO 3, TOTALING 1½ POUNDS)

Asian meatballs and fishballs (you can find these in the freezer section of Asian grocery stores; larger Asian markets may have them in the butcher's department)

Clams (Geoduck)

Crab legs

Fish, cut into bite-sized chunks

Lobster

Mussels

Scallop

Shrimp

Squid

Very thinly sliced lean beef, lamb, chicken, or pork (ideally each piece should only take 30 seconds to 1 minute to cook)

VEGETABLES (CHOOSE 5 TO 6, TOTALING 2 POUNDS)

Assorted fresh mushrooms

Baby bok choy

Bean sprouts

Broccoli florets

Chinese broccoli (gai lan), cut into 3-inch lengths

Chinese greens (yu choy, choy sum), cut into 3-inch lengths

Green beans

Napa cabbage, cut into 1-inch pieces

Snow peas

Spinach

Thin daikon slices

Tomato wedges

Watercress

OTHER

Egg dumplings, wontons, dumplings (you can make these yourself on page 81, or find them in the freezer section of Asian markets)

Asian noodles, cooked and drained

1½ quarts vegetable stock (page 11)

2 cups water mixed with 2 cups vegetable stock (page 11) in a pitcher

Soon enough, the entire family bursts into fits of giggles, and in the end we all ditch the individual baskets and just dump the entire batch of food in the pot to share, family-style. Now that is a meal we all love.

Here's what you'll need for the ultimate hot pot party:

- *Portable butane stove: You can find this at any Asian grocery store, hardware store, or online. They are cheap—about $20! Butane cartridges are about the size of a can of hairspray and will last quite a while. Get several cartridges—you don't want to run out in the middle of a meal! These portable stoves are great to have for emergencies or camping. Another alternative (and more fuel efficient) is a portable induction burner. Fagor makes a relatively inexpensive one for around $100; just make sure you have a pot that is induction friendly. We use an electric hot pot specifically designed for this meal; there's one made by Aroma Housewares for around $30 (model ASP-137).*

- *Large, wide pot to cook in (an ideal size would be 4 inches deep and 14 inches wide, like a wok or deep sauté pan).*

- *Little wire hot pot baskets or small ladles for each person. The wire hot pot baskets can be found at most Asian supermarkets. Otherwise, you can use small slotted ladles.*

- *Dipping sauces: Hot sauce or any of the dipping sauces in the Pickles & Sauces chapter (page 26).*

- *Small dishes—and lots of them: The ingredients are placed in the dishes all around the table to share. These are also good for dipping sauces.*

continued

being the last is the smartest position to have. Without a basket to watch over (to ensure the meat doesn't overcook), I'm free to use nimble chopsticks and quick eyes to snag, steal, and swim for stray nuggets of food that have floated free from the baskets, especially from Scott, who always seems to overfill his basket.

The problem is, these very light baskets have no lid, and when you try to submerge the thing in wildly bubbly, boiling broth, it ends up bobbing recklessly this way and that. Which is why the crick in the handle is important to latch onto the edge, though most of the time it proves ineffective.

There's nothing more disappointing than lifting up my basket that once held a full catch, only to have it come up with barely a scrap that resembles nibbled bait, while my husband snickers in delight next to me.

The quiet and calculating game of "You snatch mine, I'll snatch yours" ensues, which quickly escalates into downright plucking of a perfectly cooked clam right from someone's chopsticks just milliseconds before it reaches their lips.

chinese hot pot party

Chinese fondue is called "hot pot." A large, wide pot of bubbling broth sits on a portable butane burner in the middle of a round dining table (round is best, so everyone has equal access to the pot) and jam-packed around the table are palm-sized dishes of every type of seafood, vegetable, and meat you can imagine, ready to cook. All the ingredients, from fresh fish, scallops, and clams to paper-thin-sliced lamb, pork, and beef are cut into bite-sized pieces that cook in a flash, sometimes with just a 15-second swirl in the boiling broth.

I arm each person with a pair of chopsticks, a little basket for cooking, and assorted dipping sauces. The delicate wire basket has a long, skinny, twisted handle. The basket handle is malleable and bendable, which is important later on. You choose the ingredients that go into your little basket: a snap pea, a rock shrimp, and maybe a bay scallop can fit in one go. Lower the basket into the hot pot and wait anywhere from a few seconds to a couple of minutes for it to cook. If you bend the handle into a hook shape, to fit the shape of the pot's edge, your hands are free to eat the previous batch cooling on your plate. And this is where the fun begins.

As my family sits around the table, my brother Jay is the first to claim his territory in the pot. He fills his basket with meat, submerges it in the hot broth, cricks the handle, and lets it hang on the edge. That's one side. He then grabs his chopsticks, spears the scallop, and lets it cook about two inches away from the basket. The space that extends from the pie-shaped wedge right in front of him to the area in the hot pot between the basket and the chopsticks belongs him. That's his way of marking his territory.

Now, Mom, Dad, my husband Scott, and I try to do the same thing. As the last person, I have to wedge my way in to claim some little spot in the pot. It may seem like I have the least advantage, but it always turns out that

To make the rice, measure about ¾ cup of uncooked rice per person. Cook rice per instructions on pages 164–165. Once the rice is cooked, spoon it out into a very large bowl. Use a spatula to gently fluff and toss the rice, being careful not to break the grains. You want to cool the rice down. Toss the rice with 1 teaspoon seasoned rice vinegar (bottled rice vinegar with added sugar) per cup of cooked rice. Cover the cooked rice with a damp towel to prevent drying out. Sushi rice is served slightly warm or at room temperature, never hot.

To make a hand roll, place a sheet of seaweed in your hand or on a clean, dry plate. Dip your fingers in a bowl of cool water and shake off the excess. This prevents the rice from sticking to your hands.

Place about a golf-ball-size scoop of rice on your seaweed and spread it out with your damp fingers so that it covers one side of the seaweed.

Place a few pieces of ingredients on the rice. Don't be too greedy! If you overstuff your sushi roll, you won't be able to get the roll to close.

Fold the bottom left corner of the seaweed up to the middle top, kind of like folding a paper airplane.

Use your hands to roll the sushi up and to the right—kinda like making a cone—until completely rolled and ingredients are enclosed.

Use a single grain of rice on the corner of the seaweed to secure it and prevent it from unwrapping.

vegetarian korean bbq

Normally Korean BBQ is for meat lovers, but the vegetables are what I love. I marinate thick slabs of eggplant, bell peppers, mushrooms, and planks of zucchini in a savory sweet sauce. We place a grill in the middle of the table and everyone grills their own dinner.

Also on the table are small plates of roasted and salted seaweed, bowls of sticky, short-grain rice, and kimchi—lots of kimchi.

For the tabletop grill, you can use a portable butane grill or a portable induction burner (see page 97 for details) and place a grill pan on top. A seasoned cast-iron or nonstick pan is best for ease of cleaning. SERVES 6

MASTER MARINADE
1/4 cup low-sodium soy sauce
2 tablespoons brown sugar (or other sweetener, like maple syrup or honey)
1 teaspoon toasted sesame oil
2 cloves garlic, finely minced
Freshly ground black pepper
1 teaspoon toasted sesame seeds

1 globe eggplant or 2 Asian eggplants, sliced 1/2 inch thick
2 portobello mushrooms, sliced 1/2 inch thick
3 zucchini, sliced on the diagonal, 1/2 inch thick
2 bell peppers, seeded and quartered
2 leeks, white part only, halved lengthwise
Cooking oil
Assorted kimchi (pages 33–35)

Korean Bean Sprout Salad (page 32)
1 head leafy green lettuce
2 cups cooked short-grain brown rice (or more if you have big eaters)
Korean roasted seaweed (sold in snack packs) or Japanese sushi seaweed

In a large resealable bag, combine the ingredients for the marinade. Add the eggplant, mushrooms, bell peppers, and zucchini. Marinate for 1 hour or up to 8 hours in the refrigerator. No need to marinate the leeks.

Position and heat the tabletop grill and brush oil on the grate. Everyone can grill their own ingredients.

To eat, place a piece of seaweed or lettuce in the palm of your hand. Add a small spoonful of rice, then a piece of grilled vegetable. Top with kimchi or bean sprout salad and enjoy!

japanese hot pot

*In the chill of winter, why not huddle with your family over a steaming pot of
Japanese mushrooms and noodles in dashi?*

*The clay pot with dashi (page 14) is boiled on a stove top and then brought
to the table. We love the Japanese mushrooms—buna shimeji, enoki, shiitake,
bunapi shimeji, maitake, and eryngii. Our pot also includes baby bok choy,
spinach, leeks, and shirataki noodles, which are slippery little guys that are
gluten free and apparently calorie free (don't ask me how that works). Shirataki can be found in the produce section, usually near the tofu. They are
precooked—just drain and discard the liquid.*

*The clay pot keeps the broth hot throughout the meal. Have chopsticks, a
bowl, and a ladle ready for each person.* SERVES 4

5 cups dashi (page 14)

1/2 cup Japanese sake (optional)

1/4 cup mirin (Japanese sweet rice wine)

1/4 soy sauce

1/4 napa cabbage, sliced

1 leek, white part only, sliced

12 ounces tofu, cut into 1-inch cubes

1 pound assorted fresh mushrooms

1/4 pound baby bok choy

2 large handfuls spinach

1 pound fresh shirataki noodles, drained (or any other cooked Asian noodle)

Shichimi togarashi, or any Asian chili powder

In a large pot, combine the dashi, sake, mirin, and soy sauce. Bring to a boil. Add the cabbage and leek and simmer for 5 minutes. Add the tofu, mushrooms, bok choy, and spinach. Cover and simmer for 3 minutes. Bring the clay pot to the table.

Just before serving, stir in the noodles, sprinkle on shichimi togarashi, and enjoy. Each person can ladle their own bowl and choose the ingredients they like.

vegetables, tofu & eggs

OF THE HUNDREDS OF VEGGIE RECIPES I have in my stash, these fifteen are my very favorite. These are the ones that are requested over and over again by my family and friends. In recent years, I've been much more conscious of the food that I serve to my loved ones: less meat and more good greens.

Our raised bed garden and ten free-roaming chickens keep our family busy and healthy. My boys' morning chores include watering the garden, letting out the hens and collecting eggs. Their evening ritual as the sun goes down is to harvest the vegetables and put up the hens.

steamed asparagus with miso-ginger butter

This recipe isn't so much about the asparagus as it is about the ginger-miso butter. I've been known to make a jar of this stuff and drizzle it on just about every vegetable I can get my hands on, especially mashed potatoes and steamed asparagus. There's just something about the natural richness of miso that is irresistible. SERVES 4

1 pound asparagus, ends trimmed
1 teaspoon miso paste
1 1/2 tablespoons melted butter
1/2 teaspoon grated ginger
1 clove garlic, finely minced
1/2 teaspoon toasted sesame oil

Fill a large sauté or frying pan with ¾ inch of water and bring to a boil. Add the asparagus and cover with lid. Steam for 3 to 4 minutes, until crisp-tender. Transfer the asparagus to a serving plate.

In a small bowl, whisk together the rest of the ingredients until the miso has dissolved. Pour on the asparagus. Serve immediately.

blackened tofu with ginger-ponzu sauce

Given the chance, I could come up with a zillion different ways to cook tofu. This is my ingredient of choice if I was stranded on an island with my wok, some tongs, and my portable spice cabinet. Tofu takes on infinite flavors and dozens of textures, depending on cooking style and spices. If you bake or deep-fry tofu, it becomes as crunchy as a crouton. Marinate compacted tofu in savory spices and you might even be fooled into thinking it's meat. Delicately pan-fried, tofu takes on a crispy texture on the outside and is soft and pillowy on the inside.

Ponzu sauce is a Japanese citrus-soy sauce and is the basis of many of my quick salad dressings and tofu toppers. You can find ponzu sauce at most grocery stores in the Asian section or a quick recipe is on page 41 if you can't find it. SERVES 4

1 teaspoon five-spice powder
Salt and freshly ground black pepper
14 ounces firm tofu, cut into 3/4-inch slices
2 teaspoons cooking oil
1 green onion, thinly sliced
1/2 teaspoon grated fresh ginger
3 tablespoons ponzu sauce (recipe page 41)

Combine the five-spice powder with salt and pepper. Season the tofu slices on both sides with the spice mixture.

Heat a nonstick frying pan on medium-high heat. When hot, swirl in the oil. Carefully slide in the tofu slices and sear 4 minutes per side.

Combine the grated ginger with the ponzu and pour on top of the tofu. Garnish with green onion slices. Serve immediately.

What, you don't travel with your spice cabinet?

baby bok choy with garlic and ginger

Everytime I cook bok choy, it reminds me of Mom's kitchen. Mom uses the combo of fried garlic and ginger as the start of so many Asian vegetable dishes—peas, bean sprouts, broccoli, Chinese spinach. One of my favorite sounds (in addition to the snappy sound of crisp lettuce) is Mom's wok-chan (metal spatula) hitting the sides of the wok when she flips, stirs, and shakes while she cooks. (I mean the food, not her!) SERVES 4

1 pound baby bok choy
2 teaspoons cooking oil
2 cloves garlic, finely minced
1 teaspoon grated fresh ginger
$1/2$ teaspoon salt
2 tablespoons water
$1/2$ teaspoon toasted sesame oil

Wash the bok choy. Snap off the outer leaves until you reach the tender center (don't discard, we'll use it all).

Add the cooking oil, garlic, and ginger to a sauté pan or wok. Turn the heat to medium. When the garlic and ginger start to release their fragrance (take care not to burn them), add the bok choy, including the outer leaves, and stir to coat with oil. Turn the heat to medium-high, season with salt, and add the water. Cover and let cook for 4 minutes, or until the bok choy is crisp-tender. Drizzle in the sesame oil and serve.

cauliflower "steaks" with ginger-soy sauce

This is what I call impressive presentation! I can't think of a more spectacular way to serve cauliflower than this—the "steaks" look like fans! It's deceptively simple: no cutting individual florets, just slice the whole thing from top to bottom. Not only is this so beautiful, but it also saves time and you don't waste any of the stem. SERVES 4

1 large head of cauliflower, very end of stem trimmed
1 tablespoon olive oil
2 teaspoons low-sodium soy sauce
2 teaspoons water
Pinch of sugar
1 green onion, finely minced
1 teaspoon finely grated ginger
2 teaspoons toasted sesame seeds

Heat the oven to 400°F. Cut the cauliflower lengthwise, including the stalk, into ¾-inch slices and place on a baking sheet. It is okay if the slices overlap a bit. Drizzle with the oil. Roast for 25 minutes, or until the tops are lightly browned in places and the stems are easily pierced with a fork.

Whisk together the remaining ingredients and pour over the cauliflower to serve.

soft-boiled eggs with pow pow sauce

Brace yourself before you take your first bite of this dish. My go-to sauce, what my kids call the "Pow Pow" sauce, is bursting with garlic, ginger, and chiles. The secret to extracting the maximum flavor and aroma from these ingredients is to "pow" them with just a little bit of very hot oil.

SERVES 4

4 eggs

POW POW SAUCE
1 green onion, minced
1 teaspoon grated fresh ginger
1 clove garlic, finely minced
1 teaspoon minced fresh chile, such as jalapeño, serrano, or Thai
1 teaspoon rice vinegar
Pinch of sea salt
3 tablespoons cooking oil

Add the eggs to a pot and add water to cover by 1 inch. Bring to a boil. When the water begins simmering, remove pot from heat, cover and let the eggs sit for 5 minutes (7 minutes for hard-boiled eggs). Remove eggs from water. With the shell still on, cut the eggs in half lengthwise and then use a small spoon to scoop out the eggs away from the shell.

For the sauce, in a heatproof bowl, combine the green onion, ginger, garlic, chile, and salt. Set aside. Heat the oil in a small pot just to the smoking point. Carefully pour the very hot oil into the heatproof bowl to explode or "pow" with the herbs. Pour the Pow Pow Sauce over the eggs and serve.

eggs with oyster sauce

Hard-boiled eggs for dinner!? You bet! Drizzle on sweet-savory oyster sauce and spice it up with the Japanese chile-pepper blend called shichimi togarashi. which translates to "seven-flavor chile pepper." In addition to the chile powder, it will often include sesame seeds, ginger, and nori (seaweed). I sprinkle the blend on popcorn, too! SERVES 4

4 eggs
1 tablespoon oyster sauce
1/2 teaspoon toasted sesame oil
1/4 teaspoon shichimi togarashi or cayenne pepper

Add the eggs to a pot and add water to cover by 1 inch. Bring to a boil. Once the water begins simmering, remove pot from heat, cover, and let the eggs sit in the hot water for 5 minutes (7 minutes for hard-boiled eggs). Remove the eggs from the hot water, reserving 2 tablespoons of the hot water. Cut each egg in half lengthwise and use a small spoon to scoop out the egg from the shell.

In a small bowl, whisk together the oyster sauce with the reserved hot water and sesame oil. Pour on top of the eggs. Sprinkle shichimi togarashi on top and serve.

roasted brussels sprouts

Brussels sprout lovers, are you out there? Of course you are! Roasting Brussels sprouts makes them nutty and sweet. The outermost leaves will crisp up! This recipe will convert anyone into a Brussels sprouts fan.

SERVES 4

2 pounds Brussels sprouts, trimmed and halved lengthwise

2 teaspoons cooking oil

1 teaspoon fish sauce (or 2 teaspoons soy sauce with a dash of fresh citrus juice)

2 tablespoons chopped fresh herbs (such as cilantro, parsley, basil, chives)

Heat the oven to 375°F. Place the Brussels sprouts on a baking sheet. Toss with cooking oil. Roast for 15 to 20 minutes. Toss with fish sauce and herbs and serve.

ten-minute thai vegetable curry

Thai curry paste is a concentrated concoction of spices, chiles, garlic, ginger, lemongrass and other aromatics. Red, green and yellow are the most popular varieties of curry paste — you can use any of these for the recipe. A small jar or can of curry paste can be found in the Asian section of your grocery store. Keep it in your pantry along with a can of coconut milk. Curry anytime! SERVES 4

1 teaspoon cooking oil
2 tablespoons Thai red curry paste (or more)
1 (13-ounce) can light coconut milk
1/2 red bell pepper, seeded and sliced thinly
1/2 yellow bell pepper, seeded and sliced thinly
1 small tomato, cut into 1-inch cubes
8 ounces firm tofu, cut into 1-inch cubes
8 fresh basil leaves, torn
Cooked rice, to serve

Heat a wok, saute pan or medium sauce pot over medium heat. When hot, swirl in the cooking oil and add in the curry paste. Fry the curry paste for 30 seconds. Pour in a couple tablespoons of the coconut milk and use a whisk to mix. Pour in the remaining coconut milk and add in the bell peppers, tomato and tofu. Bring to a simmer and cook for 5 minutes. Taste and whisk in more curry paste if needed. Mix in the fresh basil leaves. Serve with rice.

carrots with sesame-ponzu vinaigrette

If you're tired of just having carrots in stews and salads, try roasting them (brings out their natural sweetness) and then toss them with a citrusy soy dressing. I came up with this recipe after staring at the same five pounds of carrots sitting in my refrigerator for three days. I had purchased a massive bag with my new juicer in mind. Well, the juicer broke after first use and the carrots remained untouched until this recipe.

Ponzu sauce is a Japanese citrus-soy sauce, see my recipe on page 48.

SERVES 4

1 pound carrots, peeled and sliced on the diagonal into $3/4$-inch pieces
1 tablespoon ponzu sauce (page 48)
1 teaspoon sesame seeds
1 tablespoon chopped green onion
$1/2$ teaspoon toasted sesame oil

Steam or roast the carrots until just crisp-tender: steam for 10 minutes or roast at 375°F for 15 to 18 minutes. In a small bowl, whisk together the remaining ingredients. Toss with the cooked carrots.

roasted carrots with ginger-honey mustard

When carrots are very fresh, it's a shame to do anything but roast them in the oven. If you can find them, use rainbow carrots in this recipe—they're like sunshine on a plate! It makes me happy just to see them. You can also use regular carrots (just make sure that any fat carrots are quartered lengthwise so they all roast evenly) or baby carrots, which don't need cutting.

Hands-on time for this dish is just 5 minutes. I don't bother peeling the carrots. Giving them a good scrub with a brush cleans them and keeps the nutrient-rich skin on. The honey-ginger glaze is so simple—no cooking required. The glaze is made in a heatproof bowl and after the carrots are roasted, I just let the bowl sit on the hot baking sheet to warm up before serving. SERVES 4

1/2 teaspoon grated fresh ginger

1 teaspoon low-sodium soy sauce or gluten-free tamari sauce

2 teaspoons honey

1 teaspoon grainy mustard

1 pound carrots, scrubbed and halved (and quartered lengthwise if large)

2 teaspoons olive oil

Heat the oven to 375°F. In a small, heatproof bowl, whisk together the ginger, soy sauce, honey, and mustard; set aside.

Toss the carrots with the olive oil and spread on a baking sheet. Roast carrots for 12 to 15 minutes, until tender. Remove from oven.

Place the small bowl with the honey mustard directly on the hot baking sheet; the heat will melt the honey mustard just enough to make it easy to pour. Add the mustard mixture to the carrots, toss to coat, and serve immediately.

simple chinese celery

Celery is a common (and cheap!) ingredient in Chinese stir-fries. It adds crunch and a clean flavor. Last summer, when Mom, Dad, and my brother Jay came to visit, Mom made a simple celery stir-fry that was so refreshing. The celery's fibrous strands are peeled away by running a vegetable peeler lightly over the stalks. They are quickly blanched and then dressed in a light soy sauce. I could eat this every day in the summer. SERVES 4

1 bunch celery, ends discarded
1/2 teaspoon toasted sesame oil
1/2 teaspoon low-sodium soy sauce

Bring a pot of water to boil. In the meantime, run a vegetable peeler down the outside of each celery stalk to get rid of the toughest fibers. Cut celery lengthwise into thirds, then into 3-inch lengths.

When the water is boiling, blanch the celery for 3 minutes. Immediately transfer the celery to a colander to prevent cooking further. Toss with sesame oil and soy sauce. You can serve this dish either warm, hot or at room temperature.

Mom serves this warm or at room temperature.

spicy garlicky tofu and broccoli

If you love Chinese Beef and Broccoli, you'll go nuts for this vegetarian version. Instead of the usual oyster sauce, I use vegetarian stir-fry sauce, which is flavored with shiitake mushrooms to get the umami that oysters give to oyster sauce.

I look for Lee Kum Kee Vegetarian Stir-Fry Sauce. If you eat seafood, Lee Kum Kee also makes an organic and gluten-free oyster-flavored sauce that contains oyster extracts. Look for Panda Green Label (the red label contains gluten.)

Chinese black vinegar is the magic sauce that balances all the flavors of sweet, salty, spicy, and zingy. Or substitute with balsamic vinegar—not the pricey aged stuff; the cheap one is actually better for this dish as it is less sweet. SERVES 4

1 cup water

1 head broccoli, cut into florets

2 teaspoons cooking oil

2 cloves garlic, finely minced

1 teaspoon grated or very finely minced fresh ginger

1 teaspoon minced fresh chile, such as jalepeño, serrano, or Thai

8 ounces extra-firm tofu, cubed

2 tablespoons Vegetarian Stir-Fry sauce (look for Lee Kum Kee) or oyster-flavored sauce (look for Lee Kum Kee Panda Green Label)

2 teaspoons water

1 teaspoon Chinese black vinegar or balsamic vinegar (non-aged)

Bring the water to a boil in a wok or large sauté pan, add the broccoli, and cover. Cook for 2 minutes, or until the broccoli is crisp-tender. Drain, set aside.

Wipe the wok or pan clean and return to the stove on medium-high heat. When the pan is hot, swirl in the oil, add the garlic, ginger, and chile and stir-fry until fragrant, about 1 minute, being careful not to burn the aromatics. Add the tofu, stir-fry sauce, water, and black vinegar and gently toss. Return the broccoli to the wok, toss and cook for 1 minute. Serve immediately.

kimchi omelet

Okay kimchi lovers, this one's for you! It's full of savory vegetables (green onion and zucchini) and the chopped kimchi inside gives it a spicy, crunchy, kick. But kimchi isn't the secret ingredient here—it's actually the mirin, or Japanese sweet rice wine, that brings it all together. The mirin gives the omelet just the right touch of sweetness to balance all of the flavors— salty, spicy, sour, savory, and a tinge of sweet. Kimchi adds the spicy and sour.

SERVES 2

2 eggs
1 teaspoon mirin (Japanese sweet rice wine)
1 teaspoon cooking oil
1/4 zucchini, thinly sliced into half-moons
1/2 green onion, green part only, cut into 1 1/2-inch
    lengths
2 tablespoons chopped kimchi, plus more for serving
Salt and freshly ground black pepper

In a bowl, beat the eggs with the mirin. Heat the oil in a nonstick skillet over medium-high heat. Add the zucchini, green onion, and kimchi and sauté for 2 minutes. Pour in the egg mixture, season with salt and pepper. Turn the heat to medium and cover skillet. Cook for 2 minutes, or until the egg is nearly set. Fold omelet in half and cook until done. Serve with additional kimchi on the side.

Omelets are not just for breakfast!

meat & seafood

I LOVE HOW ASIANS COOK WITH MEAT—it's a very balanced approach. Beef, pork, lamb, and chicken are almost always sliced thinly and incorporated into a dish with loads of vegetables. In stir-fries, a tiny bit of meat can stretch to feed a family of four. Choose lean meats like pork tenderloin, flank steak, and ground chicken breast.

Seafood is enjoyed abundantly in our home. Simple and unfussy preparations are the best. Make sure you try the Chinese style poached or parchment fish, you'll love how healthy and easy it is to prepare.

stuffed miso eggplant

I'm lucky enough to have one of my best friends, Kelly, cook with me once a week for my blog. She was my first friend when we moved to Florida. Thank goodness for her friendship—she was the one who inspired my cooking bug and encouraged me when I started Steamy Kitchen.

This recipe is inspired by Kelly's mom. SERVES 4

2 Japanese eggplants, about 8 ounces each (or 1 large globe eggplant)

1/2 onion, diced

1 clove garlic, finely minced

1/2 pound lean ground beef (or a combination of ground chicken and ground turkey)

1 tablespoon cooking oil

1 tablespoon miso paste

1/2 teaspoon mirin or honey

1 sprig of fresh basil

Heat the oven to 375°F. Slice each eggplant in half, lengthwise. Use a teaspoon to scoop out the meat of the eggplant into a large bowl. Set aside the eggplant "boats." Add the onion, garlic, and ground beef to the eggplant in the bowl.

Heat a large frying pan over medium-high heat. When hot, swirl in the oil. Add the beef mixture and sauté for 5 minutes, or until the beef is no longer pink. Stir in the miso paste and mirin. Cook 1 minute longer.

Set the eggplant halves on a baking sheet. Spoon the ground beef mixture into each eggplant half. Roast for 20 minutes or until the eggplant is cooked through. Top with basil and serve.

thai squid with basil sweet and sour sauce

Squid (or calamari) is one of the easiest types of seafood to cook! I know some of you may be intimidated by squid, but you can buy it already cleaned, so that all you need to do is rinse and pat dry. Thread them on a skewer, grill, and serve with a Thai-style dipping sauce that will make your taste buds sing.

SERVES 4

SWEET AND SOUR SAUCE
2 tablespooons rice vinegar or white vinegar
2 teaspoons sugar
1 1/2 tablespoons fish sauce
1 teaspoon toasted sesame seeds
Minced fresh hot chile
1 tablespoon minced fresh Thai basil

1 pound squid, cleaned and patted very dry
2 tablespoons cooking oil
Salt and freshly ground black pepper

Soak 12 bamboo skewers in water. Heat the grill on high heat or heat the broiler with the rack 8 inches below heating element. In a small bowl, whisk together all the ingredients for the sauce. Toss the squid with the oil and season with salt and pepper. Thread the squid on the skewers.

To grill the squid, cook over direct heat for 3 minutes per side, or it until it begins to curl. To broil, place the squid on a baking sheet and broil 4 minutes per side, or until lightly browned and the squid begins to curl. Serve with the sauce.

cantonese-style poached fish

This is my shortcut version to Chinese steamed whole fish. This poached version is topped with the same gingery soy sauce that you'd find in authentic Chinese restaurants. Chinese prepared fish is one of the dishes that I crave the most when I visit my parents. The fish is prepared very delicately to preserve its light, flaky texture. SERVES 4

1/4 cup low-sodium soy sauce
1/2 teaspoon sugar
1/2 teaspoon toasted sesame oil
2 tablespoons chopped fresh cilantro
3 cups water
1 (4-inch) piece fresh ginger, thinly sliced
2 green onions, cut into 2-inch lengths
1 pound fish of your choice (cod, halibut, snapper, tilapia)
1 fresh chile of your choice, sliced (optional)

In a microwave-safe bowl, whisk together the soy sauce, sugar, sesame oil, and cilantro. Microwave for 30 seconds.

In a wok or large sauté pan with lid, add the water, ginger, and green onion. Bring to a simmer and turn the heat to low. Carefully add the fish to the wok, cover and cook until the fish is opaque and flakes easily, 4 to 8 minutes, depending on the thickness of the fish.

Use two spatulas to carefully transfer the fish to a serving plate. Pour the soy sauce mixture over the fish, top with cilantro and fresh chiles, and serve.

chinese-style parchment fish

Traditionally Chinese fish is steamed whole and presented head, tail, and all at the table. It's quite a big (and messy) affair, and wrangling and scaling a whole fish can be intimidating. I've adopted a French technique for cooking fish in parchment paper and added my usual Chinese herbs and seasonings. It cuts the cooking time and makes clean up as simple as crumpling up paper and tossing it in the compost.

SERVES 4

1 green onion, halved, white part only, sliced lengthwise
1 (4-inch) piece of fresh ginger, peeled and julienned
1 (10-ounce) skinless fish fillet, such as cod, tilapia, salmon, or grouper
Salt and freshly ground black pepper
1 small bunch cilantro
1 tablespoon Chinese rice wine or dry sherry
1 fresh chile of your choice, sliced (optional)
2 teaspoons low-sodium soy sauce or gluten-free tamari sauce
1/4 teaspoon rice vinegar or freshly squeezed lime or lemon juice
Pinch of sugar
1/4 teaspoon toasted sesame oil
2 sheets of parchment paper or tin foil, 18 inches long

Heat the oven to 450°F. Position the parchment paper on a baking sheet in the shape of a cross, one on top of the other. In the center, make a bed for the fish with the green onion and half of the ginger. Season the fish with salt and pepper on both sides and lay it on top of the herb bed.

Top the fish with half of the cilantro. Fold and crimp the parchment into a packet. So that the wine doesn't pour out, carefully reopen the top of the packet, pour in the wine and recrimp tightly to make a seal. You can also use a stapler to securely seal.

continued

chinese-style parchment fish, continued

Bake for 12 to 15 minutes, until the fish is cooked through and flakes easily with a fork. If you are cooking more than one packet, add 1 minute to the cooking time for each additional packet. Just before serving, carefully open the packet, being careful of the hot steam that will escape, and discard the cilantro on top.

Top the fish with the remaining cilantro, ginger, and the chiles. Combine the soy sauce, vinegar, sugar, and sesame oil and pour over the fish. Serve immediately.

kung pao chicken

This dish is for my husband, who loves kung pao anything! He orders it anytime we go out to eat Chinese food, so I decided to make a version that was infinitely healthier and tastier. The vegetables are still crunchy-tender, and the roasted peanuts and spicy dried chiles add the "pao." SERVES 4

10 ounces boneless, skinless chicken breasts, cut into bite-sized pieces
2 teaspoons low-sodium soy sauce
1/2 teaspoon cornstarch
2 to 3 dried red chiles
2 teaspoons cooking oil
2 cloves garlic, finely minced
1 red bell pepper, cut into 1-inch dice
3 tablespoons fat-free vegetable (page 11) or chicken stock (page 10)
1 tablespoon Chinese black vinegar or non-aged balsamic vinegar
1/3 cup chopped, unsalted roasted peanuts

In a bowl, combine the chicken with 1 teaspoon of the soy sauce and the cornstarch. Marinate for 10 minutes. In the meantime, soak the dried chiles in hot water for a few minutes and when softened, chop. You can discard the seeds if you want it a little less spicy.

Heat a wok or large sauté pan over high heat. When hot, swirl in the oil and add the chicken. Spread the chicken out all over the surface of the pan. Sear on both sides until lightly brown, but not cooked all the way through, about 4 minutes.

Add the chiles, garlic, and bell pepper. Stir-fry until fragrant. Add the remaining 1 teaspoon of the soy sauce, the stock, and vinegar. Bring to a simmer and turn the heat to medium-low. Cook for 2 minutes, or until the chicken is cooked through. Top with roasted peanuts and serve.

Pao! Pao!

lemon chicken

If you've had lemon chicken before at a Chinese-American restaurant, forget about it, it's too sticky sweet. My version is all about tasting the fresh bell peppers, silky chicken breast, and the zing of fresh ginger and lemons. Once you've tried this one, you'll never go back to the sticky stuff again. SERVES 4

2 tablespoons soy sauce

1/2 teaspoon toasted sesame oil

1/2 teaspoon cornstarch

10 ounces boneless, skinless chicken breasts, cut into thin, bite-sized pieces

2 tablespoons cooking oil

1/2 of each red, yellow, and orange bell peppers, seeded and julienned

1 clove garlic, finely minced

1 teaspoon grated fresh ginger

1 lemon, preferably Meyer, zested then juiced

1 tablespoon honey

In a bowl, combine 1 tablespoon of the soy sauce, the sesame oil, and cornstarch; add the chicken and set aside.

Heat a wok or sauté pan over high heat. When hot, swirl in 1 tablespoon of the oil. Add the chicken and cook for 1 minute undisturbed. Flip and cook 1 minute longer. Transfer chicken to plate and set aside.

Turn heat to medium and swirl in the remaining 1 tablespoon of the oil. Add the bell peppers and stir-fry for 1 minute. Add the garlic and the ginger and stir-fry for another 30 seconds. Add the lemon zest, lemon juice, honey, remaining 1 tablespoon of the soy sauce and the chicken. Cook for 3 minutes, or until the chicken is cooked through. Serve immediately.

miso cod

There's a famous chef named Nobu Matsuhisa who popularized miso marinated cod—one of the to-die-for dishes at his restaurants all over the world. The nutty miso is a perfect match for any type of fish, especially buttery, rich cod.

This signature dish is a simple recipe with lots of flexibility. The fish (I use cod, but you can use any fish your little heart desires, such as salmon, tuna, snapper, or tilapia) is marinated in miso paste either for a couple of hours up to 2 days in the refrigerator. Then it's bake, broil, or grill—up to you.

Shiro miso is white miso, the mildest of all the miso pastes. You can substitute any other type of miso, but decrease the amount to 1½ tablespoons.

SERVES 4

2 tablespoons shiro miso
   (white miso)
2 tablespoons sake
2 tablespoons mirin (or
   1 tablespoon honey mixed
   with 1 tablespoon water)
1 tablespoon sugar or honey
4 pieces black cod (about
   6 ounces each)

Combine the miso, sake, mirin, and sugar in a resealable bag. Mix well. Add the fish fillets to the bag, seal the bag, removing as much air as possible. Massage the bag a bit, spreading the marinade all over the fillet. Refrigerate for 2 hours or up to 2 days.

Heat the oven to 400°F. Line a baking sheet with parchment paper. Remove the fish from the marinade and use a paper towel to gently wipe off any excess marinade, but don't rinse the fish. Discard marinade.

continued

miso cod, continued

Place the fish in the prepared baking sheet and bake until the fish flakes easily, about 10 to 12 minutes. Move the fish to the top rack and place 6 inches from heating element. Turn oven to broil to brown and caramelize the fish, about 1 minute. Keep a close eye on it as it will burn easily. Serve immediately.

sake-steamed mussels

Fresh mussels cooked simply are the best. These are steamed in Japanese sake with loads of fresh aromatics: ginger, garlic, shallots, and Thai basil. You can also make this dish with clams or shell-on shrimp.

Our good friends Wendy and Shawn live close by with their two four-legged "kids" Nakita and Dakota (who both love to swim in our pool and play frisbee). All four of them are usually over at least once a week—the dogs go crazy over hearing, "Let's go to Aunt Jaden and Uncle Scott's house!"

Wendy and Shawn love their seafood, and I've made mussels many times for them. Sometimes we'll stir in a bit of spicy Thai curry paste (same recipe, just whisk in 1½ tablespoons curry paste with the aromatics), and sometimes we relish in simplicity with just Japanese sake. SERVES 4

2 pounds fresh mussels

1½ cups sake or dry white wine

2 teaspoons finely grated fresh ginger

2 cloves garlic, finely minced

1 shallot, sliced into very thin rings

1 handful fresh basil leaves

Scrub the mussels under cool water, discarding any with broken or cracked shells.

Heat a large sauté pan, deep soup pot, or wok over high heat with the sake, ginger, garlic, and shallots. When the mixture comes to a boil, add the mussels and cover. Cook for 5 minutes, or until the mussels open.

Toss in the basil and serve immediately.

salmon-honey teriyaki

This is one of my "bag recipes": open a resealable bag, add all the marinade ingredients, throw in the fish, close, and slosh the marinade around the fillet. When you're ready to eat, take out the fish and slap it on a hot grill. SERVES 4

3 tablespoons low-sodium soy sauce
3 tablespoons mirin (Japanese sweet rice wine)
3 tablespoons sake
2 tablespoons honey
1 pound fresh salmon fillet
2 teaspoons cooking oil

Combine the soy sauce, mirin, sake, and honey in a resealable bag. Add the salmon and mix to coat. Refrigerate for 1 hour or up to 8 hours.

Remove salmon, reserving the marinade. Heat a frying pan or sauté pan over medium-high heat. When hot, swirl in the oil. Sear salmon, 2 minutes per side. Turn heat to low and pour in the reserved marinade. Cover and cook for 4 to 5 minutes, until cooked through.

My favorite bag recipe!

mapo tofu

This recipe was a staple in college; not only did my roommates love this Chinese homestyle dish, but it converted countless tofu virgins into tofu worshippers. The soft tofu cubes take on the flavors of the ground meat and oyster sauce. Spice it up with homemade Sriracha sauce (page 42) and serve over rice.

For a vegetarian version: substitute 1 cup finely chopped fresh mushrooms for the ground meat. For a gluten-free version: use GF oyster sauce. SERVES 4

2 teaspoons cooking oil
1/2 onion, diced
1/4 pound ground turkey, chicken, lean ground beef, or pork
2 cloves garlic, finely minced
1/2 cup vegetable stock (page 11)
1 tablespoon oyster sauce
14 ounces firm tofu, diced
2 cups frozen peas and carrots
1/4 cup water
1 teaspoon cornstarch (or other thickener of your choice)
1 green onion, chopped
Hot chili sauce, such as My Sriracha Sauce (page 42)

Heat a sauté pan or wok over medium-high heat. When hot, swirl in the oil, add the onion and cook for 2 to 3 minutes, until onion is softened and translucent. Add the meat and use your spatula to stir and break up.

When the meat begins to lose its pink color, add the garlic and stir-fry for 1 minute. Stir in the stock and oyster sauce and bring to a simmer. Add the tofu and peas and carrots. Cover and cook for 2 minutes.

In a small bowl, whisk together the water and cornstarch. Stir this mixture into the pan and let cook for 2 minutes longer. Stir in the green onions and season with the hot sauce, to taste. Serve immediately.

Tofu virgins watch out!

sweet and sour pork

In line with my style of cooking fresh, vibrant flavors, I've created a sweet and sour dish that is lighter in texture, brighter in color, and good for you. I've seen restaurants serve sweet and sour dishes with a thick sickly-sweet sauce that literally glows in the dark, and trust me when I say that this version beats theirs hands down. SERVES 4

For my husband, who loves sweet and sour anything!

SWEET AND SOUR SAUCE
1/4 cup freshly squeezed orange juice
1/4 cup ketchup
2 tablespoons honey or agave nectar
1/4 cup white vinegar
2 teaspoons grated fresh ginger
1/4 teaspoon salt

PORK
10 ounces lean pork tenderloin, cut into very thin strips
1 1/2 tablespoons cooking oil
1/2 red bell pepper, cut into 1-inch chunks
1/2 green bell pepper, cut into 1-inch chunks
1 tomato, cut into 8 wedges
6 ounces fresh pineapple, cut into 1-inch chunks

In a small bowl, whisk together all of the ingredients for the sauce.

Heat a wok or large sauté pan over high heat. When hot, swirl in 1 tablespoon of the oil. Add the pork to the pan in a single layer. Cook for 1 minute. Flip the pork and cook for 1 minute longer; the pork should be seared on both sides but not fully cooked in the middle. Remove from the pan.

Turn the heat to medium-high and swirl in the remaining ½ tablespoon of the oil. When hot, add the bell peppers, tomato, and pineapple. Stir-fry for 3 minutes.

Pour in the sweet and sour sauce and bring to a simmer. Turn the heat to low, add the pork, and cook for 3 minutes, or until the pork is cooked through.

noodles
& rice

THE HEART OF ASIAN COOKING is rice and noodles. If I've been traveling, the first thing I make when I get home is either steamed rice or a bowl of noodles! I've also been known to just eat both plain with nothing else, as comfort food has no rules.

Rice is flexible—you can cook it in a pot or microwave, use left-over rice in a fried rice, form it into patties to fry (page 67), serve it alongside any dish featured in this book, and even spoon some cooked rice into any soup to make it a meal.

An interesting tidbit—while most Italian pastas are made with the same ingredients (flour, egg, olive oil) but with many different shapes (spaghetti, rotini, macaroni), Asian noodles are completely the opposite. They can be made from soy, buckwheat, flour, potato starch or rice, but almost all are the similar shape, long, thin noodles.

steamed rice

White rice, red rice, brown rice, black rice—so many different types of rice! Luckily the cooking techniques for rice are very similar. Steamed rice is technically boiled and then steamed. The rice grains are first cooked in boiling water and as the water is absorbed by the grains, it produces enough steam to finish cooking the rice. Simply put: water + rice in a covered pot over fire = cooked rice = dinner.

These directions are for cooking rice in a regular old pot. (If you have a rice cooker, it might have come with a little measuring cup, which is actually three-quarters the size of a standard measuring cup, so the measurements will be different for you. I know, confusing.) **SERVE 4 TO 6**

1½ cups white rice
2¼ cups water

Pour the rice into a saucepan.

This next step is essential and often overlooked: washing the rice. It gets rid of excess starch, dust, and anything else that's "not-rice" (like a weevil or two . . . don't panic if you find them, a couple may float up in the water as you're washing, just let them pour out with the water). Fill the saucepan of rice with water, enough to cover the grains. Use your hands to swish this way and that, rubbing the grains gently. The water will get cloudy. Now slowly tilt the saucepan and pour the water out without letting the grains go down the drain. Repeat this two to three more times until the water is less cloudy. If you're waiting for the

HOW TO COOK RICE IN THE MICROWAVE

For white rice only (such as basmati, jasmine, or sushi rice). Make sure you use a microwave-safe container—there are plastic steamers that are inexpensive, or you can use a glass dish. It should be deep, at least 4 inches and come with a lid.

Scoop the desired amount of rice grains (for 4 people: 1½ cups of rice) into the microwave-safe container, pot, or steamer. Fill the pot with water and swish the water and rice with your hands. Pour out the water, keeping the rice in the pot (just cup your hands around the rice to prevent it from pouring out). Repeat for 2 to 3 more times until the water is just barely cloudy. Add enough water to cover the rice by about 1 inch. Microwave on high for 9 minutes. Let rest covered for 3 minutes.

water to be clear, you'll be washing rice until bedtime. After washing, drain as much water as you can from the pan.

Add enough water to cover the rice grains by 1 inch. You can use the "Asian finger measuring method" (see below) or a ruler if you must. Turn the heat to high. When the water begins to boil, turn the heat to low and cover. Set your timer for 15 minutes. When the timer goes off, take the saucepan off the heat (still covered) and let sit for another 5 minutes, or until you're ready to eat.

FINGER MEASURING METHOD: *Many cookbooks will give you specific measurements for both the rice and water. There's an easier method that my dad taught me. Instead of using a measuring cup, Dad would wash the rice first, then add enough water to cover the rice grains by 1 inch. No rulers here, just use your finger. From fingertip to your first knuckle is about 1 inch. Stick your finger straight down into the rice, fingertip touching the TOP of the rice grains (do not stick your finger all the way down to the bottom)—the right amount of water should reach your first knuckle.*

pineapple-crab fried rice

When I have the patience to pick crabmeat, I'll sit down with either Dungeness or blue crab, turn on the television, and go at it. It's not the most efficient way to get crabmeat, as more often than not, it's one bite for me, one chunk for the bowl. Most of the time, I just buy cooked crabmeat that comes in a plastic tub, refrigerated or frozen. Beware of canned crab as the metal can give the crab a metallic flavor. SERVES 4

2 tablespoons cooking oil
2 eggs, whisked
1 green onion, finely minced
6 ounces cooked crabmeat
6 ounces fresh pineapple, diced
1 teaspoon grated fresh ginger
2 cups leftover cooked rice, grains separated with a fork
1 1/2 tablespoons fish sauce or low-sodium soy sauce, plus more to taste

Heat a wok or large sauté pan over high heat. Swirl in 1 tablespoon of the oil. When hot, add the eggs and quickly scramble. Remove from the wok and set aside.

Swirl the remaining 1 tablespoon of the oil into the pan. Turn the heat to medium-high and add the green onion and stir-fry for 30 seconds. Add the crab and pineapple. Stir-fry for 1 minute, letting the pineapple caramelize a bit. Add the ginger and stir-fry for 30 seconds.

Stir in the eggs and rice. With a spatula, toss the ingredients and then spread the rice over the surface of the pan. Turn the heat to high and let cook, undisturbed, for 2 minutes. Toss the rice well, spread over the surface of the pan again, and cook, undisturbed, for 2 minutes longer.

Add the fish sauce, toss very well. Taste and add fish sauce or soy sauce if needed, and serve.

seafood fried rice

Here's the rule for fried rice: use leftover rice from the day before, so it's had a chance to dry out a bit in the refrigerator. Otherwise, you'll end up with goopy, heavy fried rice. I dutifully pray to the fluffy, light, airy fried rice goddess nearly once a week. It's how we use up leftover rice, and, in fact, I purposely cook more rice than I need just to have fried rice the next day. Before you cook the fried rice, separate the cold grains with a fork, it will make stir-frying much easier. SERVES 4

2 tablespoons cooking oil
2 egg whites
1 green onion, minced
6 ounces raw shrimp, peeled, deveined, and chopped
6 ounces bay scallops
1 teaspoon grated fresh ginger
2 cups leftover cooked rice, grains separated with a fork
1 cup frozen peas and carrots
1/2 teaspoon toasted sesame oil
1 1/2 tablespoons fish sauce or low-sodium soy sauce, plus more to taste

Heat a wok or large sauté pan over medium-high heat. Swirl in 1 tablespoon of the cooking oil. When hot, add the egg whites and quickly scramble. Remove the eggs from the wok and set aside.

Return the wok to medium-high heat and swirl in the remaining 1 tablespoon of the cooking oil. Add the green onion and stir-fry for 30 seconds. Add the shrimp, scallops, and ginger and stir-fry for 30 seconds.

Stir in the eggs, rice, and peas and carrots. With a spatula, toss the ingredients and then spread the rice over the surface of the pan. Turn the heat to high and let cook, undisturbed, for 2 minutes. Toss the rice well, spread over the surface of the pan again, and cook, undisturbed, for 2 minutes longer.

Pour in the sesame oil and fish sauce and toss well. Taste and add fish sauce or soy sauce if needed, and serve.

fried brown rice

This is the perfect fried rice for lunch. Not only does it include nutty, whole-grain brown rice, but also the edamame punches up the protein and fiber without adding any meat. Oyster sauce provides the savory flavor; use mushroom sauce for a vegetarian version.

SERVES 4

2 tablespoons cooking oil
2 egg whites or 2 whole eggs, if you prefer
2 green onions, minced
1 bell pepper, diced
2 cloves garlic, finely minced
2 teaspoons grated fresh ginger
1 cup cooked, shelled edamame
3 cups leftover brown rice, grains separated with wet hands
1 tablespoon low-sodium soy sauce
2 tablespoons oyster sauce

Heat a wok or large sauté pan over high heat. Swirl in 1 tablespoon of the oil. Add the eggs and quickly scramble. Remove the eggs and set aside.

Swirl in the remaining 1 tablespoon of the oil and turn the heat to medium-high. Add the green onions and bell pepper. Stir-fry for 1 minute. Add the garlic, ginger, and edamame. Stir-fry for 30 seconds.

Turn the heat to high and add the egg and rice. With a spatula, toss well and spread the rice over the surface of the pan. Cook, undisturbed, for 2 minutes. Toss the rice well, spread over the surface of the pan again and cook, undisturbed, for 2 minutes longer.

Add the soy sauce and oyster sauce and toss well. Let cook for 2 minutes longer. Taste and add additional soy or oyster sauce if needed. Serve immediately.

vietnamese rice vermicelli bowl

Rice and noodles are my comfort food, so naturally this dish is a homerun for me. Luckily with so many fresh vegetables and herbs it's also healthy and refreshing. This noodle dish is the ultimate in terms of texture and flavor notes. The noodles are warm, the lettuce and vegetables are cool, and the peanuts crunchy. The sauce is spicy, sour, sweet, and savory, all at once, in perfect harmony.

Consider this your base version. You can add grilled tofu, thinly sliced grilled meats, or seafood. See variations below recipe. **SERVES 4**

1 pound dried rice stick noodles

SAUCE
3 tablespoons sugar or other sweetener
$^3/_4$ cup warm water
3 tablespoons freshly squeezed lime juice
2 cloves garlic, finely minced
4 tablespoons fish sauce
$^1/_2$ teaspoon chili-garlic sauce, such as sambal oelek (or more to taste)

$^1/_2$ head of leafy lettuce, julienned
1 cucumber (preferably Japanese or English), julienned
2 carrots, julienned
1 cup bean sprouts
1 handful fresh mint
1 handful Thai basil
$^1/_2$ cup unsalted roasted peanuts, chopped

Bring a pot of water to a boil. In the meantime, soak the rice noodles in warm water for 10 minutes. When the water boils, cook the noodles for 30 seconds and drain immediately in a colander.

In a bowl, whisk together the sauce ingredients.

Divide the noodles, vegetables, and fresh herbs evenly among 4 large bowls. Pour the sauce evenly over each bowl of noodles. Top with peanuts.

VARIATIONS: Use the tofu from Vietnamese Summer Rolls with Grilled Tofu (page 91) or pork from the Vietnamese Summer Rolls with Roast Pork (page 89) to top these noodles.

vegetable and egg ramen noodle soup ·····································

Every day we get at least six eggs from our chickens, so I'm always looking for ways to use up our fresh eggs. I jazz up ramen noodles with a poached egg and Chinese vegetables from the garden. Cook your noodles in a separate pot from your stock because dried noodles often leave behind a starchy, cloudy residue.

SERVES 4

12 ounces dried ramen noodles (or noodles of your choice)
8 cups dashi (page 14) or vegetable stock (page 11)
6 ounces leafy greens (such as baby bok choy, spinach, Chinese broccoli)
4 eggs
6 tablespoons miso paste
1 handful nori (roasted seaweed strips)
1 green onion, julienned

Bring a pot of water to a boil. Cook the noodles according to the package instructions. Drain and divide among four large bowls.

In a separate pot, bring the stock to a simmer. Add the vegetables and cook until crisp-tender. Use a strainer to remove the vegetables and divide them among the four bowls.

Crack an egg into a small bowl or ramekin. Return the stock to a simmer, turn the heat to low, and carefully slide in one egg at a time to poach. Don't overcrowd the eggs. Let cook, undisturbed, until the whites have firmed but the yolk is still liquid, about 5 minutes. Use a slotted spoon to remove and add the cooked egg to each bowl.

Turn off the heat and whisk in the miso paste. Pour the stock evenly over each bowl of noodles. Garnish with nori and green onion.

dan dan mien

Of all the noodle dishes in the book, this is my boys' favorite. They call it "Chinese Spaghetti"! They'll each slurp up a bowl bigger than their heads and then ask for seconds.

Dan Dan Mien originates from Sichuan, China, an area known for its searing, mouth-numbing spicy dishes. Traditionally this noodle dish is served in what I call "chile soup," a broth so hot that it makes you cry just looking at it. I've toned down the recipe so that people could enjoy it without tears. SERVES 4

8 ounces dried noodles (I use egg noodles)

SAUCE

2 tablespoons low-sodium soy sauce

1 tablespoon Chinese black vinegar or non-aged, tart balsamic vinegar

1/2 teaspoon cornstarch

1/4 cup cool water

2 teaspoons hot chili-garlic sauce, such as sambal oelek (or more to taste)

1/2 teaspoon toasted sesame oil

1 tablespoon cooking oil

8 ounces ground chicken or turkey white meat

8 ounces napa cabbage, julienned

3 green onions, chopped

2 cloves garlic, finely minced

1 teaspoon finely grated fresh ginger

Cook noodles according to the package instructions, drain, and set aside.

In a bowl, whisk together the sauce ingredients and set aside.

Heat a wok or large sauté pan over high heat. Swirl in the oil and when hot, add the meat. Stir-fry until browned, about 2 minutes. Add the cabbage, green onions, garlic, and ginger. Stir-fry 1 minute.

Add the noodles and pour in the sauce. Toss until heated through and serve.

singapore rice noodles

Okay, so this dish didn't doesn't actually come from Singapore, and I have a sneaking suspicion that it was created and named by the same troublemakers that invented chop suey and egg foo yong, both American hacks on Chinese food. And by the way, I *love* hacks, which is why I love this dish. Despite the sketchy origins of this dish, with its combo of tingly warm curry powder and loads of ginger, this rice noodle dish is a fan favorite.

Last year, my husband surprised me on my 40th birthday with, "honey, pack your bags for a surprise trip!" He flew me out to Vegas two hours later. Sneaky sneaky Scott arranged to have our close friends and family jump out of a corner with a "SURPRISE!" After nearly 2 minutes of speechless shock, I screamed and laughed so loud while hugging them all, I think I triggered security. Anyway, that evening, we ordered Singapore Rice Noodles to celebrate my 40th—noodles signify long life and it's a must for birthdays!

For a vegetarian version: Omit the shrimp and substitute vegetarian oyster sauce or mushroom sauce for the oyster sauce. SERVES 4

1/4 pound thin rice stick noodles (dried)
1 cup vegetable stock (page 11)
3 tablespoons soy sauce
2 tablespoons oyster sauce
2 tablespoons curry powder (I use Madras brand curry powder)
1 teaspoon brown sugar, honey, or agave nectar
2 tablespoons cooking oil
1/2 pound shrimp, peeled, deveined and patted very dry
1/2 onion, peeled and thinly sliced
1 red bell pepper, thinly sliced

continued

japanese soba noodles

When we lived in San Francisco, our house was only a couple of miles from Japantown (though it took nearly 30 minutes to get through traffic!) and every Sunday, we'd head out to do our grocery shopping and enjoy a little lunch at the noodle joint. During the summers, soba was my noodle dish of choice; the buckwheat noodles were served with a light, savory dipping broth in a teacup and a little dish of add-ins. I'd use chopsticks to stir in a little wasabi, grated ginger, and minced green onions to the broth. To eat, I'd hold the teacup in one hand, take a chopstick-full of noodles, dip into the broth, and slurp up!

You can use instant dashi in this dish, which is just stirred in with water. Instant dashi comes in easy-to-dissolve granules and is sold in packets or a jar. To make your own dashi, see page 14. SERVES 4

DIPPING SAUCE
2 cups prepared dashi (page 14)
1/2 cup low-sodium soy sauce
2 tablespoons mirin (Japanese sweet cooking wine)
1 pound dried soba noodles

CONDIMENTS
1 green onion, minced
1 handful finely julienned nori (seaweed)
1 teaspoon finely grated fresh ginger
1 teaspoon wasabi

For the dipping sauce, combine all the ingredients and divide evenly among 4 small bowls.

Fill a large bowl with ice water and set aside. Boil the soba noodles according to the package instructions. Drain and immediately add the noodles to the ice water. Drain again and serve immediately with the dipping sauce and condiments.

sweets & libations

INSTEAD OF SUGARY SWEETS, I grew up with sliced orange wedges or tea to end the meal, which was the perfect way to cleanse the palate.

I've included in this chapter some of my very special concoctions that I love to enjoy anytime during the day. These herbal teas and infusions are simple and nourishing. In many Asian cultures, fresh fruit and tea are enjoyed for dessert. It's not only healthier but also better for your digestion to limit your sugar at the end of the meal. I often send my boys out to the garden with a small basket to "pick something for Mommy's tea!" There's nothing better than being comforted by a healthy, warm tonic that you've grown yourself.

There are times when I crave something sweet. During the summer, my ice cream maker and blender get used a lot. I love fruit sorbets and ice creams—just a spoonful in the midafternoon for an instant sweet treat.

ASIAN GOOD-FOR-YOU HERBAL INFUSIONS

Anytime I was sick as a little girl, Mom always had a Chinese herbal infusion ready, which she trusted more than popping pills. Sometimes the infusions were so bitter I had to hold my breath, squeeze my eyes shut, plug my nose, think happy thoughts, and gulp. Other times they were quite pleasant, like ginger with mint or preserved kumquat with honey (which does wonders for sore throats).

Asian herbal infusions are part of my afternoon ritual, though I leave out the strange, bitter concoctions. Usually I'll have one of the kids venture out in the backyard garden and pluck whatever herbs they feel like that day. Sometimes they'll come back with a spiraling vineful of mint and others days a few calamansi limes and Thai basil. All is good.

Today, after the light morning shower typical of south Florida, this is what called out to me in the garden: raindrops clinging to the somewhat rough, slender leaves of lemongrass and the kaffir lime tree, which is starting to bear bumpy, green fruit.

I don't use the lemongrass leaves or the fruit of the kaffir, but instead the lemongrass stalk and the kaffir lime leaves only. Add ginger slices and hot water and infuse for 5 to 10 minutes. This makes a clean, lemony "tea" that soothes and refreshes at the same time.

mom's preserved kumquat and honey

Whenever my throat got a little scratchy or sore, Mom always made me a warm "tea" of water, preserved kumquat (like preserved lemon), and honey. The warm water and honey soothed my throat and the salty kumquat killed the bugs. You can make your own preserved kumquat (it's easy, see the recipe that follows) or buy it at Chinese markets. It's usually in the snack aisle near the salted plums or in the tea aisle. In addition to using preserved kumquat as a remedy, you can use it just like you would preserved lemon in Middle Eastern or Moroccan dishes. I love adding a few inside the cavity of a roast chicken. SERVES 1

PRESERVED KUMQUATS
2 pints kumquats
1/4 cup kosher salt

Hot water
1 teaspoon honey

TO MAKE THE PRESERVED KUMQUAT: Make a little slit in each kumquat. Alternate layers of kumquat and salt in a large glass jar with a tight-fitting lid. Pack and squish the kumquats in. Cover with the salt. Cover with the lid and let sit on counter for a few days, turning the jar over occasionally. Refrigerate and turn the jar over occasionally. Store for up to 6 months.

Add 2 or 3 preserved kumquats to a cup. Use your fingers or a teaspoon to mash them up a bit. Pour in the hot water and honey. Stir and serve.

lemongrass, ginger, and kaffir lime herbal infusion

If you don't have kaffir lime leaves, you can use a regular lime. With a vegetable peeler, peel off three large strips of lime zest. Use your fingers to twist the lime zest a bit to release its flavors and aroma. SERVES 6

3 stalks lemongrass, bottom 6 inches only, tough outer layers removed, and halved lengthwise
1 thumb-sized piece of ginger, peeled and sliced 1/8-inch thick
6 kaffir lime leaves or 3 pieces lime zest (see headnote)

Use the back of a blade of the chef's knife to roughly hack and bruise the lemongrass stalk a bit. Crush kaffir lime leaves in your hand or tear each leaf in several places to release flavor and aroma.

Place all ingredients in a teapot, thermos, or other heatproof vessel. Add 1 quart of almost-boiling water. Infuse 5 to 10 minutes. You can replenish water and infuse up to 3 or 4 times.

cardamom, cinnamon, and ginger herbal infusion

This herbal infusion hits the spot when I've got a little chill in my bones — it instantly warms me up inside and out. SERVES 6

3 to 4 cardamom pods (either black or green)
3 cinnamon sticks
1 thumb-sized piece of fresh ginger, thinly sliced
1 quart water

Add all ingredients to a saucepan and bring to a boil. Turn off the heat and let steep for 10 minutes.

passionfruit mimosa

Have you ever bought passionfruit? It's round, brown, and wrinkly (if ripe)—not really an impressive looking fruit! But once you cut it open, its crimson skin shows off sunset orange fruit and edible black seeds. You'll love it with sparkling wine. You can find passionfruit juice right next to the OJ. SERVES 4

2 passionfruit, cut in half
8 ounces passionfruit juice
1/2 bottle sparkling wine or Champagne
mint, for garnish

Scoop out the yellow fruit and black edible seeds of the passionfruit. Divide the fruit and juice between four glasses. Top with sparkling wine and garnish with mint.

kiwi sorbet

Fuzzy kiwis are so fun to eat—I like to cut them in half without peeling them and use a spoon to scoop out the happy green fruit. The crunchy black seeds provide a beautiful contrast in this bright green sorbet.

MAKES 1 PINT

7 to 8 kiwis
Juice of 1 lemon
1/2 cup Simple syrup (recipe on page 198)

Remove the peel from the kiwis. In a large bowl, combine the kiwi with the lemon juice and simple syrup. Use a potato masher to mash well. Churn in an ice cream maker according to manufacturer's instructions.

Happiness will bring you
good luck.

good-for-you body and soul fortune cookies

Most of the fortune cookies I get have cheesy sayings or lucky lottery numbers, but every once in a while, I'll unfurl the little slip of paper and find something inspirational. Those are gems. My favorite fortune ever was "Every mighty oak starts as a little nut." I've kept this fortune on my desk for years! I asked my assistants, Adam and Joanne, to help me create a recipe for fortune cookies to make at home and insert your own inspirations.

The secret to making fortune cookies is to shape the cookies quickly. The batter hardens almost immediately after coming out of the oven. Make these cookies two at a time until you are comfortable with the shaping process.

MAKES 10 TO 12 COOKIES

2 egg whites

1/2 cup sugar

1/2 cup all purpose flour, sifted

Pinch of salt

2 tablespoons cream

1/2 teaspoon vanilla extract

1/2 teaspoon almond extract

2 tablespoons unsalted butter, melted and cooled slightly

Nonstick cooking spray

10 to 12 fortunes

Heat the oven to 375°F. Set up your cookie-shaping station: place a clean dish towel on the work surface along with a clean coffee cup, offset spatula, and a 12-cup muffin tin.

continued

good-for-you body and
soul fortune cookies,
continued

Beat egg whites and sugar in a large mixing bowl with a handheld mixer on medium speed until combined, 30 to 45 seconds. Add flour and a pinch of salt then beat until combined, 30 to 45 seconds. Add cream, vanilla extract, almond extract, and melted butter and beat until smooth.

Generously spray a dark, nonstick cookie sheet with cooking spray. Place about 2 teaspoons of batter onto one half of the cookie sheet. Use the back of a spoon to spread the batter into a thin 4-inch circle. Repeat with another 2 teaspoons of batter on the second half of the baking sheet. Bake 5 to 7 minutes, or until the edges turn golden brown.

Working as quickly as possible, slide a spatula under one of the cookies and transfer to the clean dishtowel. Add a fortune to the middle, then fold the cookie in half, pinching at the top to secure. Lift the folded cookie and gently press the middle of the cookie onto the side of the coffee cup to form the fortune cookie shape. Transfer the cookie to a muffin tin cup to cool. Then shape the second cookie. Repeat with the remaining batter.

mango brûlée

This recipe is inspired by one I saw years ago in the Martha Stewart Everyday Food *magazine. I serve it for a light dessert anytime I can get my hands on fresh mangoes, especially the smaller, thinner champagne variety that are creamy, smooth, and incredibly sweet.* SERVES 4

2 mangoes
1/4 cup turbinado or raw sugar
1/8 teaspoon ground ginger
1/4 teaspoon ground cinnamon
Pinch of ground nutmeg

Turn on the broiler. Position the rack 6 inches below the heat source. Line a baking sheet with foil.

Cut through the mango on either side of the pit as evenly as possible. In a small bowl, combine the remaining ingredients and sprinkle on top of each mango slice. Place the mango slices on the prepared baking sheet. Make sure the mango halves are level so the sugar does not spill out. If you need to, use crumpled tin foil to steady the mango.

Broil for 3 minutes, or until the sugar has caramelized. Alternatively, you can use a crème brûlée torch to caramelize the sugar.

carrot-ginger juice

Remember when your parents told you carrots help you see better, like a rabbit? Well, it's true! Carrots are abundant in vitamin A, which helps strengthen your eyes, bones, and teeth. We add a chunk of fresh ginger to give the carrot juice a little spicy kick.

SERVES 1

4 carrots
1 apple
1 thumb-sized piece of ginger, peeled

Using a juicer, juice the carrots, apple, and ginger. Pour into a glass and enjoy!

cucumber-mint water

This is possibly the most refreshing drink in the world! When we first bought our new house, the air conditioner decided to give up the moment the ink dried on the purchase contract. Expensive parts had to be ordered and during that crazy hot week in July, we were stuck with giant fans. The only relief we had was our swimming pool and Cucumber-Mint Water.

MAKES 1 QUART

4 cucumbers
1 handful fresh mint
1 lemon or lime
3 1/2 cups water
Ice

Using a juicer, juice the cucumber, mint, and lemon. In a pitcher, whisk the juice with the water and serve over ice.

orange-mango smoothie

In Florida, there's always a glut of oranges and mangos at the market. I keep my eye out for the honey or champagne mango, which has smooth, yellow skin and is smaller than the popular fat red/green mangos which can be very fibrous. The honey or champagne mangos have thin skins and small seeds, and the fruit is smooth, silky, and so sweet!

SERVES 2

2 oranges, peeled
1 mango, peeled and seed removed
1/4 cup plain organic yogurt
6 ice cubes

Process all ingredients in a blender until smooth. Pour into a glass and enjoy!

sparkling vietnamese limeade

There are two must-try Viet-namese beverages—the first is iced coffee (café sua da) and the second is sparkling limeade (nuoc chanh). It's minty, tingly, sour with just the right amount of sweet-ness. Instead of making a simple syrup in a sauce pan, we just dissolve the sugar in hot water, right in the pitcher or glass. Rim the glass with sea salt. Psst . . . if you like a little somethin' somethin' in your drink, a shot of gin goes great in this too! SERVES 4

2 tablespoons granulated sugar
1/2 cup very hot water
1 handful of fresh mint
8 limes
Sea salt or kosher salt
Sparkling water

In a small bowl, whisk together the sugar and the hot water until the sugar dissolves. Place a few mint leaves at the bottom of a pitcher and crush with a muddler or large wooden spoon. Juice the limes into the pitcher, add the sugar-water. Fill 4 glasses with ice and rim with salt. Pour in the limeade and top with sparkling water.

ingredients

VEGETABLES

BEAN SPROUTS The sprout of the mung bean and are one of the quickest vegetables to cook! Just a minute in the wok or blanched and it's ready to eat. Look for white stems that snap! No soggy stems. Wash the bean sprouts, discarding any that look a little soft or sad. Use a salad spinner to spin dry, store them in a plastic bag with a dry paper towel. Store refrigerated for up to 3 days.

BOK CHOY I love cooking with the beautiful spoon-shaped leaves of this Chinese cabbage; the stalks are mild and crunchy while the leaves taste like cabbage.

MUSHROOMS, DRIED Chinese Black Mushrooms are smokier and deeper in flavor than the fresh version. They are generally large and meaty and are sometimes used by vegetarians as a "meat substitute". These can be stored for a long time in your refrigerator or pantry. To use, soak them in water until soft. The thick mushrooms must be soaked for several hours. If you're in a hurry, microwave them in hot water. Start with 7 minutes and check. When I know I'll be using dried mushrooms in a dish, I'll actually soak overnight. The soaking water is flavorful (discard the sediment at the bottom) and you can use when steaming vegetables, making rice, or just adding to the pot when making soup.

MUSHROOMS, FRESH There are many different types of fresh mushrooms. Clockwise, from top: Trumpet (large/meaty, slice in half lengthwise for grilling or sauté, slice stems into "coins" for stir fries.; Enoki (thin, delicate, and long, great for soups and hot pot); Portobello; White; Shiitake (nutty flavor, hearty texture); in the center is Maitake (crunchy, holds up shape well)

TOFU Made out of soybeans, tofu is categorized by firmness. Soft, or silken tofu is incredibly delicate and you can use it cubed in miso soup. Medium and firm tofu are perfect for baking, stir frying, and pan frying, as they hold up better in the cooking process. Tofu has very little taste on its own, so it takes on whatever flavors you have in the dish. It's healthy and inexpensive to buy. It doesn't last long in the refrigerator, though, so use within a few days of purchase. Tofu often comes in a plastic tub covered with a thin plastic film. Slit the film and drain all the water out. To store, you can put the tofu in a bowl or container, fill with cool water, cover, and refrigerate. Soft or silken tofu also comes in a paper carton that does not need to be refrigerated until opened. It's much smoother and more delicate than the tub version.

BEAN SPROUTS   BOK CHOY   MUSHROOMS, FRESH   TOFU

HERBS/AROMATICS

CHILE POWDER OR FLAKES Asian chile powder is dried chiles ground into powder or flakes. It's very popular in Korean dishes and it's the heat that powers kimchi! Use sparingly at first, taste and then add more as needed. A little goes a long way, trust me. Oh, and one more thing. After you taste, wait 30 seconds before you add more chile powder. Some chile powder sneaks up on you, and its effect won't be apparent until a few seconds after you swallow! The powdered seasoning mixture, sometimes labeled as "chili powder," is used to make chili con carne should not be substituted for Asian chile powder.

CHILES, DRIED You can find whole dried chiles at most Asian markets. Soak them in hot water for a few hours and then blend with some garlic or other seasonings to make a great chile sauce, or you can throw them whole into your cooking. Of course, if you use them whole, you'll get the lovely flavor of chile without all the heat. I like to cut each dried chile in half,

empty out and discard the seeds and add the halved chiles to my dish. This way, my kids aren't surprised with a zinger if a seed (the source of most of the heat) is hidden in their food!

CHILES, FRESH Of all the aromatic ingredients, these are the most fun to play with. There are so many different chiles from all over the world and each has different levels of heat. In the U.S. you'll find everything from finger-length chiles (medium spicy) to Thai bird's-eye chiles, which are tiny but will have you screamin' for your mama. Here's my tip: Use what you like and what you can find fresh in your markets. Generally (and I really do mean generally) the larger the chile is, the less spice it packs. I try to find larger chiles because while I enjoy the flavor of fresh chiles, my spice tolerance really isn't that high. Jalapenos, while not Asian, are super-fresh and plentiful in my markets and I also grow them in my backyard. If you prefer even less heat, go for the big, fat banana peppers, which are incredibly mild but still have wonderful flavors.

CHIVES Chives are in the same family as onion, but you eat the tall, skinny leaves instead of the bulb. Chinese chives are flatter, wider, and have a more garlicky taste than other varieties.

CILANTRO (CORIANDER) The most consumed fresh herb in the world, Asians use the leaves as well as the stems.

FIVE SPICE SEASONING Chinese five spice seasoning is a mixture of fennel, star anise, cinnamon, cloves, and Sichuan peppercorns. There are different spice blends and sometimes with more than five spices. It balances all 5 flavors of Chinese cooking: sweet, salty, bitter, sour and pungent. Just a pinch is all that's needed—it's a strong spice and can take over the entire dish if you use too much! It's great when mixed with sea salt to season chicken for the grill or just a few dashes can be added to any Chinese stir-fry.

CHILE POWDER   CHILES, DRIED   CHILES, FRESH   FIVE SPICE SEASONING

GINGER   GREEN ONION   LEMONGRASS   SHALLOT

GINGER Used extensively in all Asian cooking, ginger has a hot, fragrant scent and flavor and can be used in both savory and sweet dishes. Peel off the brown outer skin by scraping it with a spoon. You can cut the ginger into "coins", thin slices on the diagonal, julienned, or my favorite way—grated. When shopping for fresh ginger, look for smooth skin (wrinkled skin means the ginger is old and dried).

GREEN ONION (SCALLION) Part of my holy trinity of Chinese cooking (along with ginger and garlic). I use green onions stir-fried with garlic and ginger as an aromatic, or sliced super thinly on the diagonal as a raw garnish. To store green onions, remove the rubber band and place them in a mason jar with a few inches of water, root side down. Cover loosely with a plastic bag.

HERBS, FRESH While most Western cooking features snipped fresh herbs as a garnish, sometimes to be pushed aside, Asian cooking features herbs as an essential part of the dish. I like to stir in fresh herbs at the very tail end of cooking, to keep their vibrancy and flavors.

To store fresh herbs, add about an inch or two of water to a mason jar and stick the herbs in the glass like a bouquet. Cover loosely with a plastic bag and keep in the refrigerator

LEMONGRASS I grow lemongrass in the backyard because I use it so much! Lemongrass is, well, a grass, that's native to Southeast Asia. Look for lemongrass that is light green and fresh looking. To use, cut the bottom 4 to 6 inches of the stalk (discard the rest) peel away the outermost layers and discard. To infuse for soups, curries: slice stalk in half lengthwise. Use something heavy to bruise the stalk just a bit to release flavors. Rings: slice the stalk into super-thin rings. Mince: run your knife through the rings, back and forth to finely mince. Grated: my favorite way is to grate the lemongrass with a microplane grater. You'll get

incredibly fine lemongrass without the fiber. I don't like lemongrass paste or powder (yuck). The frozen stuff is not bad, but I'd rather substitute with lemon peel.

MINT This herb is so flexible—it can be used in savory dishes, desserts, cocktails, and teas. It's refreshing and brightens any dish.

SHALLOTS Sweeter and milder in taste than onions, they are a very popular ingredient in Asian cooking. You can add them to your stir-fry along with the garlic and ginger, or you can deep-fry them for a crispy topping on a dish. Store shallots in a cool, dry, well-ventilated place, just as you would store your onions or garlic. Substitute shallots with finely minced onion.

THAI BASIL This variety has a stronger taste than the sweet basil that you find in supermarkets. It has purple stems and beautiful purple flowers that look great as a garnish. Substitute sweet Italian basil if you can't find Thai basil.

NOODLES

Dried Noodles:

BUCKWHEAT (SOBA) NOODLES These mushroom-colored thin noodles, which are popular in Japan, are made from buckwheat flour. It's usually served chilled with dashi-soy-mirin dipping sauce (yum) or in a hot broth.

EGG NOODLES/RAMEN This pale yellow noodle is made of eggs and wheat. They are available fresh, frozen or dried. The dried egg noodles are dried in little bundles or coils. You'll have to soak them in warm water to loosen the coils before cooking.

MUNG BEAN NOODLES These slippery noodles are made of mung beans and are gluten free! White when dried and clear when cooked, they are also known as glass noodles or cellophane noodles. They can also be deep-fried (my kids' fav!) and they magically puff up in just a few seconds time and are great as a topping for salads or a stir-fry. They come in little bundles.

POTATO STARCH NOODLES These Korean noodles are also sometimes called glass noodles and are also gluten free as they are made from sweet potatoes. The noodles are called *dangmyeon* in Korean and are grayish in color when dried; they transform to clear when cooked.

RICE NOODLES/ VERMICELLI Dried rice noodles are made from, you guessed it, rice. They come in different thicknesses, from angelhair thin to linguine thick. Soak the dried rice noodle in warm water for 10 minutes. Then dip in boiling water for 10 seconds. That's all it takes to cook! Take care not to over cook them, they become soggy and break apart.

UDON This is a Japanese wheat-based noodle used in stir fries and noodle soups.

RICE NOODLES

UDON NOODLES

EGG NOODLES

Fresh Noodles:

FRESH NOODLES These are my favorite noodles of all time, especially the wide rice noodles used in a Chinese stir fry. They don't keep that long—they'll dry out in the refrigerator, so use quickly or freeze. Fresh noodles are sold in plastic bags or containers and are found in the refrigerated or freezer section. The noodles are very quick cooking, and perfect for a last minute stir-fried noodle dish.

SHIRATAKI NOODLES (not shown) these are thin, slippery, low carb noodles made from the root of an Asian plant called konnyaku, a member of the yam family. They are healthy, gluten free, and virtually calorie free!

RICE

There are so many different types of rice—jasmine, short grain, broken, sweet, brown, red and even black! The most popular rice is the long grain, though I prefer jasmine and short grain (used in sushi and popular in Japan and Korea). Long grain Asian rice (not basmati), popular in China and Southeast Asia, is fluffier when cooked and the grains separate better. Jasmine rice (popular in Thailand) has a beautiful aroma. Short grain rice is starchier, stickier, and heartier. When mixed with a bit of seasoned rice vinegar, its texture is perfect for sushi, which requires the rice grains to stick to each other to form a ball. Before cooking rice, rinse in cool water to get rid of excess starch and to clean the grains.

WRAPPERS

NORI Japanese for thin sheets of dried seaweed, nori is usually sold in sealed packets of ten to fifty sheets. Their crispness doesn't last long once you open the package. If you have a gas stovetop, turn on the flame, take one sheet of nori and wave it over the flame to toast the seaweed for a shatteringly crisp texture. Nori also comes in other shapes—smaller squares and thin julienned strips. I love to sprinkle seasoned nori on soup, plain rice, french fries or popcorn. Seasoned nori is usually seasoned with salt, and you'll see that right on the package.

OTHER WRAPPERS From egg rolls to summer rolls and potstickers to firecracker shrimp, Asians love to wrap their food! Wonton Wrappers: Find wonton wrappers in the freezer section of an Asian market. They are very thin and square. To defrost, place package unopened on the counter for 45 minutes, or overnight in the refrigerator. Do not attempt to submerge the wrapper package in warm water or microwave to defrost. It doesn't work well

ASSORTED RICE

NORI

OTHER WRAPPERS

that way. Once the package is opened, always keep the wrappers covered with a barely damp paper towel to prevent the edges from drying. If they do happen to dry, you can just trim off the dried edges. Potsticker Wrappers: Same info as above, but they are round instead of square. They are also called gyoza wrappers. Egg Roll Wrappers: Same info as above, but they come in large squares, 9 inches by 9 inches (23 x 23 cm). Look specifically for spring roll wrappers or egg roll wrappers. Where I live, my local non-Asian market has fresh egg roll wrappers for sale in the produce section. I generally recommend not buying these fresh "pasta sheets" that are marketed as egg roll wrappers. They are way too thick and taste too starchy. You want very thin egg roll wrappers that crisp up beautifully.

VIETNAMESE RICE PAPER is translucent and brittle when dried. Once dampened it becomes soft and stretchy, and is used to roll Vietnamese summer rolls (sometimes called spring rolls). Take care not to soak them too long in water (just a quick 5-second dip). My favorite brand for summer rolls is "Three Ladies"; it's a bit thicker and better quality than the others. Look at the ingredients on the package, and don't get the ones that include "tapioca" as an ingredient—they are micro-thin and very difficult to handle. See Vietnamese Summer Rolls with Roast Pork (page 89) for more information on how to use and handle.

SAUCES & CONDIMENTS

CHILE SAUCE Made from a blend of chiles and other ingredients such as garlic, salt, vinegar and sugar. The most popular versions in the U.S. are Sriracha (see page 42 for my version of Sriracha) and Indonesian sambal oelek—a chile-garlic combo. A staple at many Vietnamese restaurants (though it originated in Thailand), Sriracha is like ketchup with a kick! I use it for everything, even as a dip for french fries (mix Sriracha with mayo). Its bottle is easy to spot—look for a green cap and a rooster logo. Sambal oelek is thicker and great to add to a bit of soy sauce for a simple dipping sauce for dim sum. I also sometimes add a spoonful of chile-garlic sauce to stir-fries. Once opened, keep chile sauce in the refrigerator.

CHINESE BLACK VINEGAR This is one of the secret ingredients in my pantry. Anytime I think a Chinese stir-fry needs a little somethin', a splash of Chinese black vinegar always does the trick. It's made with sweet rice that has been fermented. You can substitute with young or unaged balsamic vinegar.

COCONUT MILK Made by squeezing the grated pulp of a coconut, coconut milk is not the same as coconut water (which is the water found when a fresh coconut is opened). You'll find coconut milk at any Asian market and mostly likely in the "ethnic" section of your grocer (which I hope one day will be obsolete and global ingredients will be found throughout the store). Coconut milk is unsweetened (not to be confused with sweet creme of coconut used for cocktails).

VIETNAMESE RICE PAPER

CHILE SAUCE

CHINESE BLACK VINEGAR

COCONUT MILK

CURRY PASTE There are many different types of curry paste: red, green, yellow and masaman. Each is made from a different combination of herbs and spices such as garlic, ginger, kaffir lime leaf, lemongrass, galangal, and of course chiles. For best flavor, fry the curry paste in a little bit of oil first to release its flavors. If you're new to working with curry paste, it's best to start with just a bit, taste, and then adjust. With coconut milk and curry paste in your pantry, you can make a fabulous seafood dish, like Seafood Curry Noodle Soup (page 181). Curry paste keeps well in the refrigerator for several months if covered.

DARK SOY SAUCE This is very different than regular soy sauce. It is aged, darker, richer, thicker, sweeter and less salty. It's mainly used in Chinese braises and stews, where the dark caramel color is a welcome addition.

DASHI / INSTANT DASHI (HON DASHI) Dashi is the backbone of Japanese cuisine, flavoring everything from miso soup to braised chicken. It's a stock made of seaweed and dried bonito flakes. Instant dashi or Hon Dashi, is used in a lot of quick home cooking in Japan. There are vegetarian versions of dashi made from dried shitake mushrooms—though I haven't found a vegetarian instant dashi.

FISH SAUCE This is an essential ingredient in my pantry. It has a nice salty-sweet flavor, and should be used very sparingly—a little goes a long way! There are several brands of fish sauce; the best one I've found so far is called "Three Crabs." Good fish sauce should be the color of brewed tea. Anything darker (like the color of soy sauce) is a lower quality brand. If you think that "fish sauce" sounds like a weird ingredient, guess what? Most of the popular Thai and Vietnamese dishes call for it! After opening, you can store fish sauce in your pantry or refrigerator.

HOISIN SAUCE This is a sweet Chinese barbeque sauce used as a dip, or in stir fries and marinades. It's dark, almost brown-black and very sweet. It's made from fermented soybeans with garlic, vinegar and sugar. Hoisin sauce is very strong—use sparingly (a teaspoon to start) and dilute with water.

KIMCHI I don't think I've ever been in a Korean family's home without seeing kimchi in their refrigerator. Kimchi, or kimchee, is pickled or fermented vegetables

KIMCHI

and there are hundreds of different kinds. The one most popular is made of napa cabbage, garlic, carrots, and lots of chile powder. It stores pretty well in the refrigerator and for me, the more it ages, the better it tastes! It's used as a spicy condiment, though I can make an entire meal out of white rice, kimchi and a few sheets of seasoned seaweed sheets (nori). Try your hand at making your own kimchi!

MIRIN This Japanese sweet rice wine is very different from Chinese rice wine or sake and it certainly is not rice vinegar. I know, it can be confusing, as all three are so similar in name! Make sure you check the bottle and look for "sweet cooking rice seasoning" or "sweet cooking rice wine." If you don't have mirin, substitute four parts sake + one part corn syrup or sugar, dissolved. If you don't have sake, then try dry sherry or dry vermouth with the corn syrup or sugar . . . and if you don't have dry sherry or vermouth, then white wine.

CURRY PASTE   DARK SOY SAUCE   DASHI   FISH SAUCE   HOISIN SAUCE   MIRIN

MISO   OYSTER SAUCE   PLUM SAUCE   RICE VINEGAR   SHAOXING WINE   SOY SAUCE   TOASTED SESAME OIL

If you don't have white wine, well then it's time to go shopping.

MISO An essential component of Japanese cuisine, miso is made from fermented soybeans. There are so many different types and textures of miso, from delicate, light, and smooth to chocolate brown with bits of soybean chunks. It's found refrigerated in Asian markets and health food stores, but I bet you can also find it in your regular local supermarket as it's becoming more and more popular. Once you open it, keep it covered and it will last up to six months in your refrigerator. The great thing about miso is that you can just take out a little scoop and make miso soup for one. White miso is called "shiro miso" and it's sweeter and less salty than the others. Of all miso, it's my favorite because the flavor is more delicate. The deeper the color, the saltier and stronger the flavor. There's really no substitute for miso.

MISO

OYSTER SAUCE Yes, it's made from dried oysters. But no, you can't really taste them! It's dark sauce, thick and smooth; salty, smoky, and slightly sweet at the same time. Oyster sauce is used to enhance the flavor of many stir-fries, noodle dishes, and braises. There is a vegetarian version made from mushrooms, too. Once opened, keep it in the refrigerator, where it will last for months.

PLUM SAUCE This sauce is sometimes called "duck sauce" because it's often served with roast duck in Chinese-American restaurants. It's a sweet, slightly tart dipping-sauce made of plums, apricots, vinegar and sugar. It's good as a dip or a substitute for sweet chile sauce, and even as a glaze for grilled chicken. Kids love it!

RICE VINEGAR There are two types of rice vinegar (also called rice wine vinegar): seasoned (or sweetened) and regular (or unsweetened). Rice vinegar is less acidic and tart than regular distilled white vinegar. Seasoned rice vinegar is perfect for dressing sushi rice or for salad dressings as it already includes sugar in the mix. Substitute the regular rice vinegar with cider or white vinegar. To make sweetened rice vinegar, take 1/4 cup

unsweeteened rice vinegar, cider or white vinegar and add one tablespoon of sugar.

SHAOXING WINE This is the most popular Chinese rice wine, made from rice and yeast. While you can drink good quality Chinese rice wine, it's not my spirit of choice. However, I can't imagine cooking Chinese dishes without it! I use Chinese rice wine in everything—from marinating meats, to a splash in my stir-fry, to an entire cup in braises. You can substitute with dry sherry.

SOY SAUCE Made from fermented soybeans plus some type of roasted grain (wheat, barley or rice are common). Choose a low sodium version. The quality of the soy sauce is important too—look for "naturally brewed" on the label—the rest are probably chemically brewed.

If you're gluten intolerant, choose gluten free soy sauce. Tamari (contains wheat) is smoother, more balanced and less salty than regular soy sauce.There are gluten-free Tamari brands as well.

TOASTED OR DARK SESAME OIL This oil has dark amber color, a very low smoking point, and a distinct aroma. Just use a few drops or a drizzle in a dish.

acknowledgments

Big hugs and kisses to my little boys who aren't so little anymore, Andrew and Nathan. Thank you for being my official taste testers and kitchen assistants. Thank you for being honest and letting me know that the "Chinese hot pot is the bestest" and telling me not to put that "icky bean recipe" in the book. To my husband, Scott, for fixing all my technical "uh-ohs", for being my best friend in the world, and for being so patient with all the seafood experiments. You're my favorite cluster of cells (remember that!?). To Coco, you are the best food guard dog ever. Thanks for not eating the photo shoot.

To my Mom and Dad, who always made dinner time a loving family moment—we always ate together every night. Thank you for your love, and for inspiring me to be the best parent I can be. To my brother, Jay. I'm not sure I deserve such an awesome brother. You've always been there for me. Always. Well, except that time you blamed me for writing on the wall with a marker when we were kids. To Mimi and Papa, I love you both, "enfiniddy."

To the Steamy Kitchen crew: Julie Deily, Kelly Hutchins, Adam and Joanne Gallagher, Cheri Parrag, and every single recipe tester who helped me refine the recipes for the book. I owe the most massive thank you to Todd, Diane, and Jenna—THANK YOU for helping with the cooking and photo shoot—the book is gorgeous because of you. To the dynamic husband-and-wife team, Salvatore and Jennifer.

To my B-town posse, Wendy and Shawn Crane, Julie Goodall, Charlie and Patsy Ugarte, Patti and Tom Carpenter, Suzanne Nolin, Isabelle Carpenter and everyone at Carpenter Taekwondo!

To all the kiddies that I love so much: Dakota, Nakita, Dylan, Drew, Jake, Sydney, Audrey, Julia, Ryan. Your hugs make me so happy!

To Elise Bauer and Ree Drummond, I don't know how I could ever blog without your friendship and sisterhood. VC girls—yeeehaaawww! Guy Michelier, I will never eat another oyster without ticking it first. To the BlogHer team; my entertainment agent, Daniel Ryan-Kinney; and attorney, Jackie Eckhouse.

Of course, this book wouldn't be possible without my agent, Janis Donnaud, editor Jenny Wapner, and the entire Ten Speed Press team.

Lastly, a massive helping of appreciation and love to all my readers and fans on the blog, Twitter, Facebook, and Pinterest. I LOVE YA!

about the author

Jaden Hair is the publisher of the award-winning blog, SteamyKitchen.com, which specializes in fast, fresh, and flavorful Asian food.

She's been featured on the *Today* show, *CBS Early Show*, Martha Stewart Living Radio, Oprah.com and in *Parents* magazine. Jaden has also been named one of the best food bloggers by Forbes.com and one of the best Mom food bloggers on Babble.com and The Daily Meal.

Her recipes are featured on TLC's Parentables and in the *Tampa Tribune*. You can watch her cook on the show, Daytime, syndicated on 120 stations.

Her first cookbook, *The Steamy Kitchen Cookbook*, was published in 2009.

measurement conversions

VOLUME

U.S.	IMPERIAL	METRIC
1 tablespoon	1/2 fl oz	15 ml
2 tablespoons	1 fl oz	30 ml
1/4 cup	2 fl oz	60 ml
1/3 cup	3 fl oz	90 ml
1/2 cup	4 fl oz	120 ml
2/3 cup	5 fl oz (1/4 pint)	150 ml
3/4 cup	6 fl oz	180 ml
1 cup	8 fl oz (1/3 pint)	240 ml
11/4 cups	10 fl oz (1/2 pint)	300 ml
2 cups (1 pint)	16 fl oz (2/3 pint)	480 ml
21/2 cups	20 fl oz (1 pint)	600 ml
1 quart	32 fl oz (12/3 pints)	1 l

TEMPERATURE

FAHRENHEIT	CELSIUS/GAS MARK
250°F	120°C/gas mark 1/2
275°F	135°C/gas mark 1
300°F	150°C/gas mark 2
325°F	160°C/gas mark 3
350°F	180 or 175°C/gas mark 4
375°F	190°C/gas mark 5
400°F	200°C/gas mark 6
425°F	220°C/gas mark 7
450°F	230°C/gas mark 8
475°F	245°C/gas mark 9
500°F	260°C

LENGTH

INCH	METRIC
1/4 inch	6 mm
1/2 inch	1.25 cm
3/4 inch	2 cm
1 inch	2.5 cm
6 inches (1/2 foot)	15 cm
12 inches (1 foot)	30 cm

WEIGHT

U.S./IMPERIAL	METRIC
1/2 oz	15 g
1 oz	30 g
2 oz	60 g
1/4 lb	115 g
1/3 lb	150 g
1/2 lb	225 g
3/4 lb	350 g
1 lb	450 g

index

To my late Gong Gong (Grandpa),
who taught me the joy of dim sum.

Text and photographs copyright © 2013
    by Jaden Hair
Photographs on pages viii, x, 39, and 150
    copyright © 2013 by Salvatore Brancifort
    and Jennifer Soos
Foreword copyright © 2013 by Ree Drummond

Published in the United States by
Ten Speed Press, an imprint of the
Crown Publishing Group, a division
of Random House, Inc., New York.
www.crownpublishing.com
www.tenspeed.com

Ten Speed Press and the Ten Speed Press
colophon are registered trademarks of
Random House, Inc.

Library of Congress Cataloging-
in-Publication Data

Hair, Jaden.
    The steamy kitchen's healthy Asian
favorites / Jaden Hair ; photography by Jaden
Hair. — First edition.
        pages cm
1. Cooking, Asian. I. Title.
    TX724.5.A1H325 2013
    641.595—dc23
                                        2012029987

ISBN 978-1-60774-270-8

Printed in China
Design by Katy Brown

10 9 8 7 6 5 4 3 2 1

First Edition